CHINESE ART

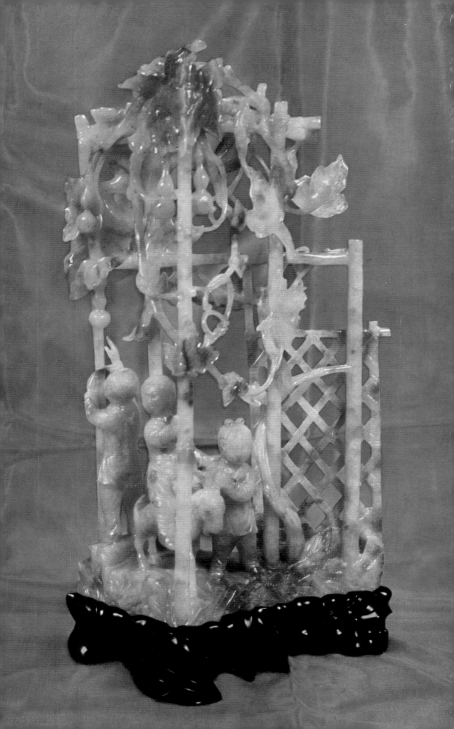

MARIO PRODAN

CHINESE ART

An Introduction

PANTHEON

Published 1958 by Pantheon Books Inc.

333 Sixth Avenue, New York 14, N.Y.

★

© Mario Prodan 1958

*Library of Congress Catalog Card
Number: 58–11711*

N
7340
P75

Manufactured in Great Britain

FOR

MICHELA, CLAUDIA & LUCA

CONTENTS

ILLUSTRATIONS

In Colour

In Black and White

11

12

FOREWORD

We wish to warn the reader that this book does not pretend to be anything more than an attempt to present, in a readable and, we hope, agreeable form, information which hitherto has been available only in volumes compiled with all the gravity proper to scientists. Nobody could be more conscious than the author of the difficulties of such an enterprise, not only because he himself has had occasion to marvel at the immensity and profundity of the facets which give life to the Chinese jewel, but also because he is by no means convinced that art, that is to say beauty, is a matter about which it is possible to write.

Anyway we have made the attempt. We embarked upon this enterprise because we felt an urgent desire to throw a little light on a subject which hitherto has been obscure and vague; to give readers a conception of the term 'Chinese art' higher than that which is produced by enamelled cloisonné basins, little ivory figures of fishermen and embroidered sleeve-bands.

The attempt will have been successful if these pages awaken in some of our readers a desire to consult the works mentioned in the bibliography, just as we have done ourselves! In these precious volumes our readers will find, in addition to a far more profound knowledge of the subject, all those references and notes which the author of this book has so unconscientiously omitted.

But that experience will no longer be a simple chance encounter. At an introduction one should do no more than converse agreeably, though certainly not foolishly. And this, too, the author has endeavoured to achieve: though he has abandoned the scientific manner of exposition, he has not hesitated to follow what is generally considered to be the scientific method of assimilation.

If the reader is willing to accept this assertion in good faith he will be able, simply by reading the book, to judge whether the attempt has been successful. And should his judgement be unfavourable, we hope that he will allow the illustrations, for which no credit is due to the author except the choosing of them, to speak with the authority which is their due, since they, of course, are far more important than the text.

M. P.

THE CHINESE DYNASTIES

SHANG-YIN   (?) 1766–1122 (?) B.C.

CHOU   (?) 1122–221 B.C.

    Early Period 1122–947
    Middle Period 947–770
    Late Period   770–221

CH'IN   221–206 B.C.

HAN   206 B.C.–A.D. 220

THE SIX DYNASTIES   220–589

SUI   589–618

T'ANG   618–906

THE FIVE DYNASTIES   907–960

SUNG   960–1279
    Northern   960–1127
    Southern 1127–1279

YUAN   1280–1368

MING   1368–1644
    Reigns   Hung Wu   1368–1398
              Chien Wen   1399–1402
              Yung Lo   1403–1424
              Hung Hsi   1425

MING—*continued*

Hsüan Te	1426–1435
Cheng T'ung	1436–1449
Ching Tai	1450–1457
T'ien Shun	1457–1464
Ch'eng Hua	1465–1487
Hung Chih	1488–1505
Cheng Te	1506–1521
Chia Ching	1522–1566
Lung Ch'ing	1567–1572
Wan Li	1573–1619
T'ai Ch'ang	1620
T'ien Ch'i	1621–1627
Ch'ung Cheng	1628–1643

CH'ING   A.D. 1644–1912

Reigns	Shun Chih	1644–1661
	K'ang Hsi	1662–1722
	Yung Cheng	1723–1735
	Ch'ien Lung	1736–1795
	Chia Ching	1796–1820
	Tao Kuang	1821–1850
	Hsien Feng	1851–1861
	T'ung Chih	1862–1873
	Kuang Hsü	1874–1908
	Hsüan Tung	1909–1912

CHINESE REPUBLIC   1912

CHAPTER ONE

The Chinese

If we wish to derive benefit from a study of Chinese art we must first of all rid ourselves of a large part of those preconceived notions which we have absorbed, bit by bit, ever since the days when our mothers taught us the meaning of the pictures in a spelling-book. In these days, now that we have succeeded in changing to a considerable extent our mental attitude towards beauty and are constantly finding ourselves confronted by points of view growing ever more complex—and to some of us terribly disconcerting—it is less difficult to do this than it was in the days when Landseer painted his portraits of dogs. But although in this age of feverish search for solutions to problems it is better to discard all mental attitudes, nevertheless, before attempting to approach the Chinese point of view, we have to assume another attitude, no less restrictive than that adopted by our artists when their work was defined and circumscribed by their faith—faith in God in whose image and after whose likeness man had been created.

It will therefore be necessary for us to study the Chinese themselves and their way of considering the problems of life and art. And it is better to start this brief voyage of discovery here—in other words to take as our starting-point the word 'faith'.

The Chinese have never believed that God created man in His own image and after His own likeness. Even if they had ever toyed with such an idea, they would inevitably have reflected that men, like cats and tigers, are tormented by inordinate desires, but of a kind peculiar to the human race, with a tendency towards so high a degree of self-worship and adulation that, if not controlled, it may well culminate in the supernatural— a result both terrifying and absurd. The only thing the Chinese really believed in was their unworthiness in the presence of Nature and their only catechism was an attempt to find in Nature a niche from which they might contemplate the grandeur of all things created. When questioned as to his views regarding the supernatural, Confucius, that counsellor of princes and founder of an ethical system which retained its validity for nearly three thousand years, replied that the supernatural is beyond all our capacity of comprehension and that worrying about it was a loss of time when compared with the urgency of discovering the best way of living on this earth. The fact that in the course of time he became a kind of divinity, and a religion was founded in his name, is more than the mere revelation of the perversity of human ignorance; it is a product of the imagination of a people, in the habit of creating, from the idea of grandeur, an apotheosis full of gods, of genii and spirits, who are nothing else but the forces of Nature in a vulgarized form. And even if the doctrinary form of Confucianism subsequently became the official State religion, another revealing element in the Chinese character is that they still go on living in accordance with the doctrines of a completely different philosophy (which comes first? A philosophy or the people who follow it?), namely Taoism, which in its turn became a religion with even more gods, genii and spirits than Confucianism!

To obtain an idea of the difference between the

Oriental and the Occidental conceptions of art, it would be useful to make a thorough study of the practical aspects of Taoism. But since we do not wish to exceed the limits we imposed upon ourselves when writing this book, we will restrict ourselves to quoting one of the maxims of the master Chuan Tze:

The life of man passes like a galloping horse, changing at every turn, at every hour. What ought he to do, or what ought he not to do, except allow his own decomposition to continue?

It is in this deep humility that we must seek the key to the art of this people. The heroic aspect of virility is not to their taste. The gigantic figures that fill the pages of the Old Testament and of our epic poems do not exist, and soldiers are there only to lament the disasters of war, cataclysmic events in human nature, like floods and thunderbolts in Nature itself. Or else we find them on the stage, behind the mask of the old general dressed in plumes and flags and puffed up with his own importance. When he opens his mouth, it is to emit guttural howls, since he always has to keep his chest properly inflated. He has a black mouth with fiercely drooping corners. In him it is easy to recognize the epitome of human stupidity.

We find no other trace of human heroism—unless we can consider as such the heroism of a faithful wife, of a father or brother who accepted every adversity with resignation. All the rest is the heroism of Nature, and of Nature alone, even when it assumes the semi-divine forms we have mentioned, of which there are so many in Chinese art: fairies and dream-creatures pregnant with allusions, emerging from magic bottles and vases which in themselves are allusive; Lohans, the Immortals, Bodhisattvas, symbols of one or of several religions, mingled together by the tolerance of people whose beliefs are only relative, to give life to an other-world of fantasy, so necessary to people who live hard lives. It must be admitted that there is a certain dose of 'queerness' in the Chinese, and also, always considering them from our point of view, of ignorance, because the 'scientific ignorance' we find in them is always remarkable. Perhaps if we examine one branch of this ignorance and try to trace its origin, we shall be able to explain its presence in other fields.

Take, for example, the Chinese ignorance of anatomy, a special kind of ignorance which many people inevitably find irritating. Was this due originally to a reluctance to unveil a mystery, a refusal to dismember the work of the Creator merely to satisfy a thirst for knowledge? (If it is possible to give a convincing rendering of a man without dismembering him, why do it?) The veneration of ancestors which protects the dead is merely reverence for a mystery; and it is important that a sage should remain on this side of the boundary, always vague and indefinite, between knowledge and super-knowledge, since on the other side of it he might find the abyss of evil.

It is precisely in this world of semi-knowledge that the Chinese have sought and found their artistic inspiration. It is from this twilight that the Chinese have created their boundless horizon, and it is in this cult of the vague that they have contrived to give the impression of a completeness more complete than anything else that can be defined in human terms. The Chinese artist moves and struggles in the midst of this mysterious twilight—sometimes in a mood of reverent awe and sometimes with bursts of passion, but always with a full acceptance of his earthly limitations. His mystery is of this earth, extending horizontally through sensual morasses, terrible and attractive at the same time, since they reflect the seasons and humours of this earth. Perhaps this image will become clearer if we consider our Mediterranean art as a precisely defined column rising vertically and meeting divinity half-way. The Mediterranean climate is propitious, but that of China is pitiless, alternately afflicting the country with floods and periods of terrible drought, natural forces with which no compromise is possible, which cannot be met half-way. Man can only converse with his immediate surroundings—with the pensive shape of a fruit or the terrifying grimace of a wild animal, with the imposing spectacle of an animal's back or the ever-present, overwhelming grandeur of a mountain, a river or a tree. The real task of an artist is to convey this atmosphere, and he gives proof of his ability when he knows how to reveal his harmony with this Nature in an instantaneous flash of sudden knowledge.

*

Another essential preliminary, in view of the circumstances, is an understanding of the public for whom the Chinese artist works. We must first of all remember that among the Chinese the appreciation of works of art was the privilege of many dead persons and of only a few among the living. We will, however, leave to the chapter on funerary art our study of artistic production in honour of the dead; here we restrict ourselves to that of works of art destined for the living.

In China poetry, calligraphy and painting—the three sublime arts—are practised by the learned for the benefit of the learned, sometimes even for the sole enjoyment of the artist himself. In ideal circumstances the artist does not sell his works to anyone. A scholar and one of the *literati*, he has become a Civil Servant, the highest social category to which a Chinese can aspire. Having passed the Imperial examinations, he becomes a member of the nobility, even if his father was a cobbler; and his son, in turn, may become a mere cobbler or, worse still, a soldier, if he cannot satisfy the Imperial examiners. In China artistic and literary activity has always been the preserve of Civil Servants, to such an extent that the time a bureaucrat dedicates to art is not only tolerated, but is looked upon as a kind of capital investment producing dividends in the form of the progress of national culture.

These *literati* therefore explore the depths of their knowledge for their own mutual enjoyment, filling their works with allusions and quotations which they alone are capable of understanding. And it is for this reason that Chinese art demands from the spectator more co-operation than the art of any other nation. Chinese artists do not need to satisfy, or even to take into consideration, the tastes of ignorant patrons. They create a pool for those who are able to swim in it, for those possessing a flair for allusions and recondite meanings which is the fruit of an essential ability—the ability to decipher and interpret Chinese characters. The difficult work of interpretation these characters demand is the whetstone on which this ability is

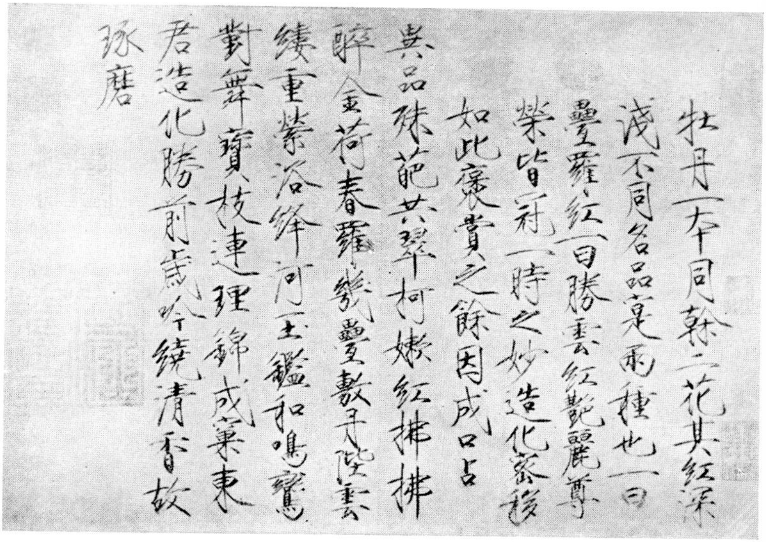

牡丹一本同榦二花其紅深
淺不同名品竟亦兩種也因
疊羅紅曰勝雲紅艷麗尊
榮皆冠一時之妙造化窠後
如此褒賞之餘因成口占

其品殊范共翠柯嫩紅排排
醉金荷春羅羅鬖疊疊陛雲
綾重縈浴絳河玉鑑和鳴鸞
對舞寶枝連理錦戍棗東
君造化勝前意吟繞清香故

琢磨

PLATE 1. Poem in the handwriting of the Emperor Hui Tsung of the Sung Dynasty (1101-1125 A. D.). *Chinese Government*.

PLATE 2. Earthenware jar, unglazed, with decorations
in red and dark brown. Yang Shao culture.
Victoria & Albert Museum, London.

PLATE 3. Earthenware *li*, unglazed. Yang Shao culture.
Height 9¹/₂ inches (24 cm.). *Ostasiatiska Samlingarna,*
Stockholm.

PLATE 4. Bronze lid of a *ho*. Shang-Yin Dynasty.
Freer Gallery of Art, Washington.

PLATE 5. *Chüeh* in bronze. Shang-Yin Dynasty. Height 8 inches (20 cm.).
Collection of His Excellency Alexandre J. Argyropoulos, Athens.

PLATE 6. Bronze axe or *ko*. Shang-Yin Dynasty. Length $9^{1}/_{2}$ inches (24 cm.).
Cleveland Museum of Art, Cleveland (Ohio).

PLATE 7. Bronze *ku*. Shang-Yin Dynasty. Height 12½ inches (31.5 cm.).
Collection of His Excellency Alexandre J. Argyropoulos, Athens.

PLATE 8. Bronze *chia*. Shang-Yin Dynasty. Height 15³/₄ inches (40 cm.).
Freer Gallery of Art, Washington.

continually being sharpened. There are, for example, no real translations of Chinese poems, because no acoustic interpretation can convey a direct image from the eye to the brain as the ideogram does. Only a Chinese character can reveal sudden glimpses of poetic visions (sometimes clear and luminous, sometimes bathed in a mysterious obscurity), which make a conclusive interpretation of an individual concept possible. A chord is struck only in the mind of one who is able to appreciate. Knowing how to appreciate is everything, if by that we mean the ability to recognize, to judge and to enjoy a sensation, a vision, a thought. For the Chinese this is the measure of civilization. Following in the wake of Confucius, they believe firmly that it is not possible to appreciate without understanding. And understanding demands knowledge—knowledge derived from culture. To Chinese ears the cut-and-dried statement that 'it is not what is beautiful that is beautiful; what pleases, is beautiful' seems nothing but a revelation of crass ignorance.

If we wish to understand the permanence of Chinese institutions, we must stress again and again the importance the Chinese attached to these *literati*. Throughout Chinese history, the sage has been the real moderator, the real ruler, and only if they understand this and adopt this system of government can barbarian invaders hope to survive. When, therefore, we speak of Chinese civilization, it is of this literary *élite* that we must speak, of the men who guided the gradual evolution of their nation for more than three thousand years. It was they, the perennial connecting links transcending revolts and invasions, who set the style and the pace. And the people, that huge mass of peasants, merchants and artisans, supplied the raw material for this *élite*, even if their influence was negligible. In reality, if we speak of Chinese art from the Chinese point of view, we should speak only of literature, calligraphy and painting, because these, and these alone, are the arts practised by the learned. If, on the other hand, we include other forms of artistic expression—the bronzes, sculpture, household and funerary ceramics—we are including things which for the Chinese themselves are merely the products of artisans.

It is difficult to explain a definite social system to those who live under a very different system. We will therefore limit ourselves to saying that in China the difference between artists and artisans is almost a difference of race. It may well happen that a learned Chinese, examining the work of an artisan of a different period, will speak of it with the same astonishment as he would if he examined, say, the intelligent work of a beaver. Nevertheless, in accordance with an established artistic criterion, both are recognized as being on the same level, since the essential difference between our conception of an artisan and the Chinese is a matter of creative ability. A Chinese potter who moulds a beautiful vase and then paints a flower on it, a flower which does not represent any known species of flower but is the very essence of all flowers, is no less an artist than a monk, who, with the blows of his chisel, gives a sense of piety and spirituality to the attitude of a Bodhisattva; and both are certainly on the same creative level as the artist who painted the landscape in Plate 47. The first may have been a peasant, the second a priest and the third a sage. The extent to which creative talent of this kind has penetrated into every social class can be appreciated only by those who are acquainted with the innumerable rungs which make up the Chinese social ladder. We can affirm without fear of being contradicted that in no other country have the stimulus and the talent for creation ever been so universal.

But we have not yet done with our artist-sage; in fact we must take a closer look at him. Since he is the product of the rigid discipline of scholarship, virtually unchanging from one century to another, it will be better if we approach him by way of his studies. However brief this examination may be, it will also have the advantage of helping us towards a better understanding of other chapters in this book. Apart from that, no book dealing with Chinese culture can afford to overlook what constitutes China's greatest monument—her literature; and that not only because of its universal value, but also because no other field of expression is more profoundly Chinese than this, or more important for the Chinese themselves. Chinese poetry is like a precious casket full of thoughts set to music, and we shall shortly give a specimen of it, for although translation necessarily weakens the effect, it would not otherwise be possible to give an idea of the strange osmotic relationship existing between poetry and painting. We shall often find ourselves referring to the 'classics'. No nation has produced more literature on art than the Chinese, and even though this may be 'non-scientific', like our art history before the pragmatic innovations of the Germans, the greater part of our knowledge of the historical aspect of art can be derived only from this literature.

*

We can affirm that the pre-eminence of the *literati* was in the main due to the invention of Chinese characters, and the fact that the development of these was so uneventful must be attributed to the soundness of the original conception (though this is a statement which might lead us to a long digression on the reluctance of the Chinese to interfere with principles). It cannot, however, be denied that only a peculiarly gifted mind could ever learn to recognize the approximately forty-four thousand characters which form the written Chinese language—this written language being totally different from the spoken language and capable of rendering a concept in less than two-thirds of the space necessary for expressing it in words. It is therefore logical that this knowledge was limited to a few people and that these few, trained in a very hard school of erudition, came to form a group apart. For the Chinese, superficial knowledge is a very dangerous thing and the conception of universal culture as absurd as would be that of universal virtuosity. A complete knowledge of Chinese characters and how to write them is in itself an unparalleled *tour de force* of erudition. The influence exercised by Chinese characters on the formation of Chinese methods, thought and art was enormous. Writing was always the ultimate test of erudition. A sage's mental aptitude was revealed not only by elaborate expositions of already accepted Confucian, Taoist or Buddhist maxims, but also, and perhaps to an even greater extent, by the visual element, by the calligraphy in which the expositions were displayed. On the basic theme of the sage-become-ancestor (and thus worthy of veneration and faithful imitation), a scholar produced variations serving to confirm and embellish the original concept, in a calligraphy which long practice had rendered fluent, but which the strength of a personal structure, acquired by confidence in his own erudition, endowed with a power all its own.

Such themes and variations predominate in Chinese classic literature—in the Chinese 'classics'. If it is true that the greatness of a nation's literature should be judged by its volume and not by the spasmodic achievement of one author, then China is undoubtedly in the front rank. This bulky collection of literary works is the training-ground of the would-be scholar, but the very vastness of the material allows him to make a choice which will enable him to express those individual tastes that will subsequently be the measure of his own peculiar talent. Among the Chinese classics there are works which deserve to be described as great; on the other hand, there are others that can hardly be called even mediocre. In a treatise on the proper conservancy of rivers, the author passes from considerations on hydraulics and engineering worthy of the admiration of a European scientist to solemn instructions on the best ways of avoiding trouble with the local water-spirit. A treatise of this kind may be included in a volume classified as 'History', together with travel diaries, biographies and descriptions of the mechanism of government. The range of arguments to be found in the Chinese classics is enormous, and although in the 'classic books' attributed to Confucius and his disciples philosophy and the art of government have the chief place, they may also be said to comprise the greater part of all human consciousness. Even the works classified as 'Philosophy' and catalogued by the Emperor Chien Lung deal with such themes as boxing, palmistry, interior-decoration, gastronomy and the art of war. Huge masses of volumes formed encyclopaedias a thousand years before the idea first occurred to Diderot and his friends. Some of these assumed such proportions that the Emperors who had commissioned them either died or ran short of funds before they were completed, but others reached their mastodontic conclusion. A lexicon of the kind, commissioned by the Emperor Yung Lo of the Ming Dynasty, eventually comprised twelve thousand tomes, each divided into two volumes.

The writing of all these works was done in 'Wen Li', i.e. the classical language of which we have already spoken. Fictional narratives as ends in themselves were considered unworthy of a literary man. Romances, dramas, folklore and short stories were therefore written in the vernacular, that is to say in the language as it was spoken, even if written by learned scholars, especially in troublous times when the government was too disorganized to employ *literati*. The *Ching Ping Mei* is a work of this kind and although it is merely the chronicle of a dissolute nobleman, the licentious subject is treated with great elegance and artistic feeling. As an interesting sidelight on Chinese moral principles, we think it worth while mentioning the excuse thought up by the writer for writing this book. We are told that he wrote it to punish one of his enemies, a dissolute man, intending to present him with his scandalous conduct in literary form. As the enemy had a taste for pornographic literature, he would read the manuscript with such avidity that he would not notice that the corner of each page had been tinged with poison, and licking his finger before turning over the pages he would die before reaching the end of the last chapter.

The *Ching Ping Mei*, one of the most widely read romances both in China and abroad, is undoubtedly the work of a scholar who, probably for the sake of the money, debased himself by using a literary form inferior to his position, just as Francis Bacon is said to have done with Shakespeare's plays.

*

It is, however, to poetry that the Chinese classics devote most space. This is the most sublime of all the arts, the treasury of all Chinese thought, and it is through it that one day it will perhaps be possible to understand the Chinese people. It is in poetry that they reveal themselves, showing all the delicacy of their attitude towards life. Even when singing of death and disaster (which they often do), the tone remains subdued and the noise of battle is no more than a distant echo. Sometimes they are intense and abrupt in the revelation of their sensuality—not sexual sensuality, but something deeper and more universal; sensations that body and mind experience in a particular atmosphere, through the desires of a particular moment. Of sex itself the Chinese have a conception very different from our own; for them it is a law of Nature and in no wise shameful, an experience in which men and women have equal shares and from which everything springs. This belief is recognized in their religious principles. But even when their poetry does become intense and direct, it is immersed in a strange vagueness, as if the moment, the situation were viewed from a certain distance. The emphatic forms of poetry are not found in Chinese literature. Of Western poets the most akin to the

Chinese is Keats, with his love for the beauties of the country, his contemplative vein of quasi-sorrow, considering joy and trouble with equal detachment.

We can form a vague idea of the amount of poetry written in China if we remember that the T'ang Dynasty alone (A.D. 618–906) has left us nearly fifty thousand poems written by more than two thousand poets. But how many other poems were written and subsequently lost? How many were destroyed by authors who wrote merely for their own delectation? The origin of Chinese poetry is lost in the mist of the beginnings of their civilization, yet even today it is the only form of culture rich in artistic expression. Mao Tse-tung himself is a poet of no mean stature, and another modern, Sun Chin-san, expresses moments of sensual desire in an idiom not unworthy of the old masters.

Amidst such abundance it is difficult to make a choice, even if one is compiling an anthology. Here we have chosen two poems with a view to illustrating, in the first, the affinity between painting and poetry, while in the second we come into fleeting and intimate contact with a personage of whom we already know, or should know, a good deal. Both poems are by Tao Yuan Ming, a fourth-century poet. A sage who became a hermit, he is perhaps the most characteristic of his type.

CHRYSANTHEMUMS

The chrysanthemums of autumn have the finest colours,
Flowers and leaves moistened with dew.
I drink this cup of wine that brings forgetfulness,
Putting to flight all earthly cares.

Alone, I raise the cup to my lips:
More wine is poured in when the cup is empty.
And at sunset all is silence,
While the birds fly back, twittering, to their nests.
Beneath the balcony I cry impetuously towards the East,
Content, now that my humble life can continue.

THE SAGE

In the East there lives a sage
Who is often without clothing and sheets.
In thirty days he takes only nine meals,
A carp he makes last for ten days.
Yet, despite all the privation and poverty,
His aspect is always serene.
I went to see him one morning,
Scaling hills and fording torrents;
Green pines fringe the road before his house
And white clouds hover above the roof.
Knowing well why I had come,
He took his lute and touched the chords.
The first note was the lament of the 'Wandering Crane',
The second evoked the grief of the 'Solitary Phoenix'.
I wish I could remain with him
Until the year exhales its last breath.

*

Such, then, were the artists, the men who created, or
by their example set the standard of that creative
production we are about to study. In the few pages at
our disposal it is not easy to give a better explanation

of their mental make-up. But there is one experiment we might try on ourselves, even though comparisons are reputed to be odious. Let us compare Plate 48 with one of our European paintings, exalting, say, a certain Messer Castruccio (full-blooded, bursting with self-confidence, set in a landscape which is admitted as background to his portrait only because it belongs to him). If, when we do that, we feel a certain pleasure, it means that we can approach Chinese art with some chance of understanding it.

CHAPTER TWO

Origin and History

According to the Chinese philosopher and historian Mencius (372–289 B.C.), the history of China is wont to move in cycles of five hundred years, in an ever recurring pattern of: (a) Domination by a foreign conqueror; (b) his absorption; (c) a period of confusion; (d) a long period of national government. For us it is not difficult to check the truth of this assertion, both before the days of Mencius and afterwards; but it is far more important to consider his assertion as an instance of the innate Chinese tendency to organize history and, very often, to mould it into a determined system. This tendency, together with that of drawing moral lessons from the past, has caused such confusion in the written history of China that it is difficult to arrive at the truth by relying on its evidence. On the other hand, attempts to make a systematic and modern study on an archaeological basis, which, by about 1930, had made considerable progress, have been interrupted by recent political events. We have still, therefore, to rely on the 'classics', those Chinese annals of only relative value from the point of view of what we call historical accuracy. The importance of this Chinese idiosyncrasy —never to inquire too deeply into a historical fact— can never be exaggerated. It is to this idiosyncrasy that we can attribute a large part of the recent upheavals, since it is owing to this attitude, which we can call 'unscientific', that the West has been able to find a means of penetrating into China. It is, for example, quite possible that the scientific refutation of Confucius' affirmation of the virtues of ancestors may have caused, in the ethical code which he established on the basis of this affirmation, a scission so great as to permit the easy penetration of a modern creed.

For the reasons given above, any study of the origins of China and her history must perforce be based on two sources: incomplete archaeological data referring only to a small portion of the country, and certain passages in Chinese historical texts which confirm these archaeological data or which, as a result of subsequent events, would seem to include a certain element of truth.

*

From the very start we find ourselves faced with a proof of the inadequacy of archaeological data. Whereas the Swedish scientist Andersson found in the environs of Peking the remains of one of the earliest specimens of the human race—the *Pithecanthropus Pekinensis* (who, it seems, was in the habit of eating his dead relations)— subsequent archaeologocial excavations in China tell us nothing until about five thousand years later, the period of those perfect clay vases of which we shall speak below. The situation becomes, however, clearer, though at the same time somewhat fantastic, when we learn that Chinese history books fill this gap by stating that Twelve Emperors of Heaven and Twelve Emperors of Earth reigned for four hundred thousand years, followed by Nine Emperors of Humanity who ruled for another forty-five thousand years, until the arts and crafts had been invented and the Imperial House had been founded.

Archaeological excavations have brought to light objects dating from epochs about fifteen hundred years apart, all of them perfectly finished and revealing no signs of the long evolution which must have been needed in order to reach such a standard of perfection, in particular the really astonishing perfection of the bronzes of the second epoch. These formidable gaps cannot be explained as being attributable only to lack of sufficient excavation. The terrain on which civilizations usually flourish is in China of a particular kind. In the vast plains traversed by rivers there has been a considerable displacement of the very fine soil known as *loess*. And it was the whims of this soil, and the fearful floods which periodically altered the course of the rivers, that must have been responsible for the disappearance of large quantities of buried material.

Be that as it may, if we confine ourselves to what we know, to the objects on which we have laid our hands, we find the first clay vessels and the earliest utensils wrought in bone in Northern China. We are immediately struck by the unusual shape, obtained by joining together three elongated vases and giving them a common mouth—an ideal solution for a stout three-legged cooking utensil. Fifteen centuries later we find the same form in bronze, in a receptacle for use during the rites in honour of ancestors. Even in the days of the earliest clay vessels, the soil was tilled, producing a species of red millet and perhaps rice as well. Pigs and dogs were bred for eating purposes. Sheep and cattle appeared in Northern China towards the end of this neolithic period, but horses were still wild and were hunted.

About the same time, in the western province of Kansu, there appeared a different kind of vase, much more delicate and embellished with beautiful and bold designs. Usually these vessels are red, but some of them are in black and white. The shapes are handsome: capacious jars for water, bowls, cups and the three-legged cooking utensils we have already described. The date attributed to this culture, known as *Yang Shao*, is about 3000 B.C., and to justify this dating we must compare these finds with others, easier to date, made in Persia and in the basin of the Danube, with which the objects we are discussing have a curious resemblance and from which it is believed they may derive. It will be as well to stress at this point that many of these deductions as to definite Western influence on the East are considered arbitrary by some modern scholars, in particular Chinese scholars, who maintain that archaeological knowledge of China is still too scanty to justify any such certainty.

The *Lung Shan* culture, likewise neolithic, was discovered in the province of Shantung and is attributed to around 2500 B.C., since it is superimposed on the *Yang Shao* in places where the two cultures occur together. The excavations made there are more important than the earlier ones, since they brought to light a large number of magnificent black vases, evidently moulded on wheels, and also because they prove the existence of a community which had reached a surprisingly advanced stage. It has been proved archaeologically that these people built houses not very different from those of Chinese peasants today, that they lived in towns and used shells as utensils. They had wheeled carts, drawn by domesticated horses.

*

It has not yet been possible to discover the link between these neolithic men and the SHANG-YIN DYNASTY (?1766–1122? B.C.), but there are grounds for supposing that this first historical period in China developed out of the neolithic by a process of evolution lasting fifteen hundred years, of which not the slightest trace has remained.

It is at this point, with the Shangs, in the vast plain formed by the southern loop of the Yellow River, that we suddenly find ourselves on surprisingly firm historical ground—firmer than that which we shall tread during our subsequent gropings through the centuries. Here systematic and comparatively scientific excavations have been made. And here, together with the incredible bronzes of which we shall speak in a later chapter, we find the first written messages, giving us a truly prodigious vision of life in those times.

But before discussing them, we must turn to the historical Chinese evidence, in quest of information concerning the period immediately preceding the Shang Dynasty, which, scientifically speaking, we have had to leave blank. On consulting the *Book of Changes* (which, being one of the oldest books, was rewritten the most) and groping our way through a veritable labyrinth of Divine Ancestors and Emperors, we learn that a people called Hsia, considered by the Chinese to be the ancestors of the Shangs, and therefore of the whole race, obtained complete possession of the northern plains of China by defeating the Miao, who, to judge by their totems of which descriptions have come down to us, must have been a seafaring people.

*

The Shang messages we have mentioned, magnificent but succinct, are found on bronze vessels, and one of these could be described as the Rosetta Stone of archaic Chinese writing, since it contains a hymn of praise to a prince translated into Sanskrit. But we obtain more intimate knowledge of these people from another source.

Towards the end of the First World War, strange bones began to appear in the antique-dealers' shops in Peking. The dealers maintained that they were dragons' bones, found in the neighbourhood of Anyang, in the valley of the Yellow River. The bones bore strange signs, the same signs that had been found on bronzes, and on closer examination cracks could be seen which might have been caused by fire. These cracks frequently seemed to have been underlined by the same pointed instrument that had engraved the characters. At first little interest was aroused and it was thought that this was merely another of the innumerable tricks to deceive simple customers. But after some time a change of attitude took place. The Chinese Government was beginning to consider requests for excavation permits received from foreigners, especially Americans, and soon systematic excavations were started in the zone which for some years past had been the undisputed territory of tomb-robbers. It was thanks to the tomb-robbers, who operated by night to avoid arousing the ire of peasants mindful of the precepts of Confucius and fearful of the vengeance of their ancestors, that European and American private collections had hitherto been able to enrich themselves by acquiring funerary relics, with Chinese dealers acting as middlemen. This gruesome trade began very late in China, not more than forty years ago. We shall see later how real Chinese art came to us from tombs, with the exception of the paintings, of which we have only copies, and of porcelain dating from after the Sung Dynasty. Consequently, when an antique-dealer tries to entice a customer by maintaining that the wares he is offering are bound to be valuable and old because they were brought out of China by a great-uncle of his who was present at the sacking of the Summer Palace during the Boxer Rebellion in 1900, the potential buyer may be certain that he will be shown terribly complicated furniture, porcelain of recent manufacture, enamelled jugs and emboidered cloaks—unless the antique-dealer is completely indifferent to historical truth, in which case it will be difficult to foresee what he will try to get rid of.

Many of these bones came to light as a result of systematic excavations in the Shang area and soon began to furnish a veritable torrent of information. It was found that the inscriptions consisted of questions put to diviners ('Will the harvest be plentiful?' 'Will the Emperor have good weather for his journey?'). From the shape of the cracks made by fire on the bones, the diviner deduced his answers ('Yes.' 'No, it will rain' —and on one bone, by way of postscript 'And it did rain'), answers which were engraved on the bone itself. Apparently these bones, usually sheep's shoulder-blades, were kept for eventual future reference, since many of them are numbered and pierced with holes as if they had been filed away.

It is naturally impossible here to give the reader all the information derived from these inscriptions. In order to throw further light on Chinese ethics, it will suffice if we say that they reveal certain circumstances

41

which we and Confucius would be inclined to call immoral: while the Imperial family, the governing class and the priests were living an intense, cruel and luxurious life, the people as a whole lived under conditions worse than slavery. The poor tilled the soil, the women wove silk; and increases in the birth-rate were encouraged by means of orgiastic fertility rites in the spring, followed in the autumn by thanksgivings which did not differ from the rites of spring. Even in those days the inspirers of these rites were the ancestors.

The ancestors inspired Imperial ritual to an even greater extent. In order to comfort the dead, it was a common practice to make human sacrifices. On the death of a prince, for example, in addition to a mass-slaughter of servants and concubines, the earth used for sealing his tomb was mingled with the blood and even the heads of newly decapitated soldiers of the guard. And apart from similar religious sacrifices, it was considered more than permissible to massacre conquered foes, except when it was held to be more convenient to keep them as slaves or as material for subsequent sacrifices when the need arose.

On the other hand, although Confucianist evidence loves to present these glorious ancestors as living under a unified government, the bone-oracles reveal that the political system of the time fluctuated between feudalism and a centralized Imperial regime, according to how much of a despot the Emperor was. Notwithstanding this, all forces were united when there was a threat of foreign aggression. Such threats generally came from the nomads of the north-west, whom the bone-oracles call 'shepherds'. The soldiery was recruited from among the peasants, most skilful not only in using, but also in making deadly bows, the arrows from which could penetrate any armour used at that time. This twofold ability remained the prerogative of the Chinese peasants for many centuries. And if the possession of weapons by the lower classes can be related to the particular social physiognomy of a nation, one might believe that the respect shown by subsequent ruling classes in China for the peasants was due more to this skill than to ethical or economic factors. Later, the bow became the *ta tao*, the Great Knife, and this, too, was usually a home-made weapon.

In any case, during the Shang period, an enormous gulf divided the nobility from the people. The nobles had already grasped the value of culture as a means of keeping the people at a distance and they made others study what they themselves were incapable of learning. One may thus say that the *literati* were born at the same time as China—first as wizards capable of interpreting supernatural signs and later as learned men entrusted with the compilation of edicts, memorials and correspondence in accomplished and elegant language which would impress their contemporaries, as well as posterity.

The Shangs, who laid the foundations of the Chinese system and institutions and were wise enough to combine the temporal and religious power in one man, ruled for more than seven hundred years and in the end were thrust from power by an internal movement, since their successors, the Chous, were vassals from the north-western frontier.

The Chous had acquired great experience in the art of governing while subjugating the barbarian nomads, and gradually, by a slow but sure process, they had annexed the territories of many other feudal barons of the Shangs, while declaring their steadfast loyalty to the Emperor. At the beginning of the tenth century B.C., Wen, king of the Chous, annexed the whole empire in the most courteous manner. After deposing the Shang Emperor, he asked the governing families to make a few small changes in the structure of government in order to conform with Chou principles— and deprived them of every possibility of recovering power. He made no other changes, because everything seemed to be functioning extremely well, especially as regards the taxing of the peasants. In fact it is probable that this was a pleasant surprise for him, since he came from a pastoral community in which the collecting of taxes must obviously have been a matter of serious difficulty.

*

To the CHOU DYNASTY (?1122–221 B.C.) belongs the honour of having built, on the foundations already laid by the Shangs, a solid and organized system of life and government. The microcosm of the family, as it has remained down to our own century, was established and consecrated by the Chous; the conception of patriarchy now became absolute. The women had no other ancestors but those of their husbands and although polygamy was also practised unostentatiously, monogamy was the law in the sense that only one wife could enjoy the important family privileges. In any case, the women received education and advised their husbands even in matters of State. Just as the 'paterfamilias' was the head of the house by ancestral tradition, so the Emperor was the head of the nation by divine will.

44

He was the Son of Heaven. The early Chou period was one of consolidation and splendour, but Shang customs still persisted as regards assassination and slavery.

Nevertheless, if considered according to Chinese ideas, this idyllic state of affairs did not last long. Although it is usual to speak of a Chou Dynasty, the absolute rule of this family did not last more than two hundred years. Provincial princelings and despots gave the first signals of rebellion against the yoke of a feeble Emperor who had ascended the throne by hereditary right, and discontent began to spread among the peasants who had to bear the burden of supplying armies growing ever larger in order to defend the country from barbarian invasions. About 700 B.C. the Emperor had to revert to a kind of Shang regime and became the 'pro-forma' head of about a dozen feudal states which, while paying verbal homage to his divine mandates, were in actual fact almost independent. Finally, before the end of the fifth century B.C., these states definitely broke away from the Emperor and thus began the so-called period of the 'Warring States'.

It was during this period of change and unrest that the great philosophies of China (strangely parallel in time to the Greek) appeared on the scene and established those directives of thought which were to remain valid for about twenty centuries. Lao Tzu, Kung Tzu (Confucius) and Mo Tzu belong to this period. It will always remain a mystery why a later Emperor should have officially adopted the teachings of Confucius in preference to those of the other great philosophers. A famous counsellor in his time, a product of that intellectual class which during the early Chou period was recruited from the populace and not from the nobility,

Confucius tried to establish order out of the chaos prevailing in the country, by giving advice to the feudal princes. As examples and as incentives to good behaviour he always quoted the Shangs and the early Chou rulers, great and venerable ancestors, making good use of the firm foundation that he, the foremost of scholars, derived from the historical knowledge of those virtuous men which he claimed to possess. These repeated references to ancestors had a distinct flavour of divinity, and ancestor-worship was in fact encouraged by Confucius. But his concessions to the supernatural do not go beyond this.

It is difficult to summarize in a few lines the teachings of the Master, yet the attempt is worth making, because his ethical system formed the basis of Chinese government for almost two thousand years, until the advent of the Republic. There is one concept that occurs again and again in his lessons: that of 'names'. Modern scholars have endeavoured to discover behind Confucius' obscure language an idea which would be more appropriate to Mussolini, namely that a bad leader is not a leader at all, that he has no right to the 'name' of leader and that, although we owe him absolute obedience and even adoration so long as he remains the leader, he must be deposed as soon as possible, presumably by means of a revolution. This concept is not applicable only to the head of the government, but applies equally to the whole social scale, obliging the philosopher to spend much time 'giving a name' to the various social categories and family gerarchies, assigning to each of them its functions and limitations. Confucius was always ready to answer any questions, and his replies, transcribed and collected, cover practically every field of human relationships. His attitude was, nevertheless, coherent, pragmatic and energetic. While others advised vague and even mystic attitudes, Confucius demanded an explanation of all functional conduct. With him, one always knew where one was and where one ought to be. Yet his prime consideration was that of the 'names' and the right of making use of them, and it is really surprising that a Han Emperor should have given official and exclusive approval to such an audacious point of view (and not at all a healthy one for a dynastic ruler). In Confucius' own lifetime his philosophy could only compete, though with a certain success, with the rival Taoism of Lao Tzu and the doctrine of love of Mo Tzu, as contrary to his own teachings as their natural mildness would allow.

*

Sanguinary and cruel wars had greatly weakened the Chinese communities. The Shang and Chou custom of massacring prisoners of war became a double-edged weapon. The barbarians from over the frontier who penetrated into the country as immigrants were rapidly absorbed, but the decimation of the noble chiefs had grave repercussions. All the feudal Chou states, except one, suffered from this weakening.

The state of Ch'in, situated in the north-western corner of the Empire, was well protected from invasions by its mountains and by its reigning house, virile and courageous. In addition to this, its half-Chinese inhabitants had always shown a great ability in exploiting immigrants for military and civil purposes. Following the advice of certain scholars who had studied in the

Legist schools, the state of Ch'in, which had previously been feudal, gradually changed its structure with a view to embarking upon a policy of conquest. The Legists were philosophers who supported the revolutionary doctrine of the equality of all men in the eyes of the law.

The immediate result of this doctrine was the disintegration of the family and its logical consequence was that the individual became more and more dependent upon the State, which gained control by means of a system not unlike that of the modern Communist cells.

Out of all these novelties there emerged the figure of Shih Huang Ti. In 221 B.C., after completing the absorption of the Chinese States begun by his predecessors, he proclaimed himself First Emperor of China. Thus the CH'IN DYNASTY (221–206 B.C.) was founded and the New Order began to function with the speed, the zeal and, alas, the shortcomings characteristic of all totalitarian regimes. The Great Wall was built, books were burned and scholar-philosophers were persecuted, especially the Confucians, whose doctrines constituted an incitement to rebellion. On the other hand Taoism, which was mild, submissive and elastic, and the Mo Tzu philosophy of universal love were treated with less severity. But huge palaces were built, a programme of public works was carried out and methods of government adopted which lasted until the end of the Empire. The Emperor was certain that his dynasty would last more than a thousand years, but after his death the whole structure fell to pieces and from the point of view of art, the period may be said to have been non-existent.

*

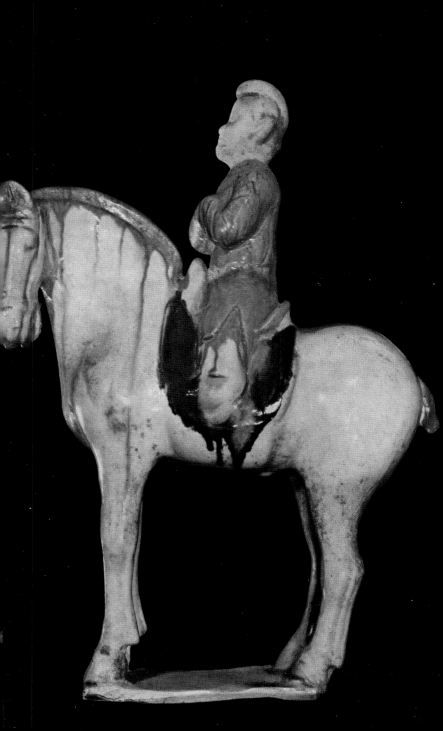

PLATE B. Horse and rider in glazed earthenware. T'ang Dynasty. Height 15 inches (38 cm.). *Collection of Contessa Margherita Tagliavia, Palermo.*

Liu Pang, the son of a peasant, founded the great HAN DYNASTY (206 B.C.–A.D. 220), after foiling the attempts of certain nobles to re-establish a feudal form of government. In quick succession, after being a brigand he became a duke and then Emperor, assigning to himself the divine right of ruling by means of a very personal interpretation of the Confucian doctrine of 'names': 'I rule well, therefore I rule.' His ability in this field cannot be doubted; totally illiterate, he was sufficiently energetic and sagacious to imbue the Empire with a strong sense of unity and to lay the necessary foundations of a dynastic government destined to last for four hundred years. Even today many Chinese still call themselves 'Han-Jen', that is to say, sons of Han. This was the first really national Chinese State and for the first time the influence of China made itself felt in the world.

In 191 B.C. Shih Huang Ti's edict against books was revoked and this was followed by a feverish search for a State philosophy and for an official point of view in ethical matters. From this period date the first copies of ancient texts. Confucianism arose stronger than ever after the persecution and the scholars, encouraged to become candidates at the Imperial examinations, the aim of which was a stricter control of them, chose the religion which had contrived to conceal its claws by means of a re-interpretation and revision of its own doctrines. The Hans accepted it and Confucianism from this time on became the official religion of China.

Taoism, however, its eternal rival, had also regained much of its vigour. While Confucianism obtained a footing among the governing class, Taoism became more and more popular among the governed, by always adapting itself to the needs of a people continually exposed to the caprices of Nature.

The period was one of great splendour in many fields. China now had a population of seventy millions, a figure which remained unvaried for a thousand years and formed, in its enormity, 'that ocean which will salt all the rivers'. This is, in fact, a great moment for a people whose greatest virtue will be a tranquil capacity to absorb every influence and stimulus coming from beyond the sea and the mountains. It is important to stress at this point the fundamental efficiency of the government at that time, already able to control and organize such a large population scattered over such a vast territory. Trade flourished in the districts around the cities and comprised the whole country, since the different areas produced their own particular products and exchanged them for others coming from every corner of the Empire. The means of communication were good, both on land and along a system of canals well adapted to the great size of the Chinese plains. As before, agriculture remained the basic activity of the community; the smallholders tilled their fields in the vicinity of the villages. The patriarchal families of the Chou period were restored by Confucianism.

The dynamism of the new State, however, was not confined to internal matters. Under the Hans new territories were acquired, including the whole of Korea to the east, the whole of Manchuria to the north and Annam to the south. To the west, beyond the deserts, Han rule extended to the frontiers of Parthia.

Contact was established with Rome and a flourishing trade in silk ensued with that Western counterpart of the Han Empire. Foreign influence consequently became more considerable, as we shall see when we study the art of the period.

In the first century of our era, the capital was removed from Ch'ang An to Loyang, where, after a short period of strife, the dynasty established itself for another two hundred years. 'Western' and 'Eastern' are the names given to the two periods, from the position of the two capitals.

*

Nevertheless a cancer that had begun to take root during the early years of the Han period finally overwhelmed the great ruling house. The eunuch had made his appearance, that phenomenon of decadence destined to recur many times in the vicissitudes of Chinese Imperial families. The reason for his power, far greater than that of his Islamic counterpart, was that whereas the latter was only a slave castrated by order of his master in his youth, the Chinese eunuch was a volunteer professional who had often fulfilled his duties of procreation before he submitted to castration. Only the lust for power could lead a man to accept such a drastic sacrifice. When these ambitious men procured Court emoluments for their families outside the palace and incited them to enter upon that hunt for benefices and bribes which has always been the sport of every courtier, the resulting rebellion contributed to the further weakening of organisms, the blood of which had already been sucked by this cohort of leeches. In A.D 220 palace conspirators brought about the fall of the House of Han and led to four hundred years of struggles between the mutually hostile States that were the product of this disintegration.

Notwithstanding this, these years were of great importance for the development of China, because, although they are wrongly called 'China's dark period', they gave birth to the most glorious of all Chinese Dynasties, that of the T'ang. Foreign influence, always salutary, made itself more and more felt and Buddhism established itself definitely.

These four hundred years are called, historically, the PERIOD OF THE THREE KINGDOMS (A.D. 221–280), whose warlike feats were afterwards exalted by dramatists and poets. It was, however, also a period of philosophical research for a means of getting away from Confucianism. Years of gallant resistance were followed by barbarian invasions and the confusion in the country became greater and greater. The native leaders were obliged to withdraw to the south of the Yang-tze and the following period was known as the SIX DYNASTIES (A.D. 220–589), such being the number of the ruling families who succeeded one another on this southern throne.

The period is very interesting on account of the Buddhist innovations in sculpture and painting. It was the golden age of Wei sculpture, inspired by a new idealism which a people yearning for happiness accepted as a revelation—the revelation that, even in times of stress, the spirit can find peace. We should not undervalue the impulse given by this new element, this religion of Buddha demanding profound spiritual exercises. And though we have only a vague intuition of its influence on the arts, it is clear that it wrought a far greater change in the people, who until then had been content to placate their ancestors and evil spirits by carrying out certain rites. From the start Buddhism was vigorously opposed by the Confucians, who saw in it a menace to their official ascendancy. But the tolerance characteristic of the Chinese and the conditions of unrest and poverty made it possible for enthusiastic Indians to carry out a vast work of propagation.

It was a general of the northern family of the Chous who, after usurping the throne from his nephew and subjugating the great Wei family, set out to conquer the other Chinese States, combining them to form a united China after four hundred years of semi-anarchy. He gave to his dynasty the same of SUI (A.D. 589–618), and his son Yang Ti raised the country to a level of great splendour in the arts and learning, as well as encouraging a rather unusual form of progress. It was, in fact, due to his direct intervention that work was begun on the Imperial Canal, that means of communication which was to join the north to the south, thus providing a unity which remained effective until the advent of Communism and is now more important than ever. Various interpretations of the Emperor's motives have, however, been put forward. If we take into account his taste for splendour as shown in the sumptuous edifices adorning his capital, Loyang, we are bound to agree to a certain extent with those who believe that the Imperial Canal was built merely because he wanted to travel. His reckless expenditure of money, and the disastrous war he undertook in an attempt to subjugate Korea, finally brought about his downfall. The States his father had subjugated rebelled, under the leadership of one of his governors, a man who was astute enough to seize power before the Empire relapsed again into anarchy. He founded the T'ANG DYNASTY (A.D. 618–906), but it was his son, the great Li Shih-Min, who made the family illustrious. Many historians consider him to have been the greatest man ever to occupy the Chinese throne, despite the fact that his interest in art seems to have been slight, perhaps as a reaction against the extravagant and munificent patronage of Yang Ti. Li Shih-Min was more of a soldier, and he was certainly a very able administrator. Under his rule the Empire extended its frontiers in every direction; the country was wisely divided up and organized into ten provinces, the system of government by scholars being revived and to some extent modified, especially as regards the examinations. As State religion and philosophy Confucianism gained more and more ground, even though this was a period of great tolerance, especially in Court circles, where Buddhism was beginning to be viewed with favour. Free access to the Court was also granted to numerous foreigners, in whose erudition and teachings the Emperor and his courtiers took a great interest. One may say that the capital, Ch'ang An, was the most cosmopolitan city in the world at that time. Business men came to its great markets from Europe, Africa, the Near East and Japan; religious and political refugees took shelter there from all manner of persecution. Christian churches were built by Nestorians, synagogues by Jews, mosques by Mohammedans. The Emperor engaged a translator to expound to him the meaning of the Christian Gospels.

The country had now entered upon a period of stability which could afford to be tolerant. The Emperors ruled serenely and for a long time, constantly faithful to Confucius' doctrine of 'names'. After the death of T'ai Tsung (the title given posthumously to Li Shih-Min), twenty-two years after his accession, his son Kao Tsung authorized his wife, the celebrated Empress Wu, to govern the country after him. The Chinese historians, all Confucianists, have little good to say about her—probably because, in addition to being a woman, whose place was therefore in the home according to the teaching of Confucius, she was a convinced Buddhist. An objective examination of the facts, however, leads one to suppose that she was at least sufficiently capable to maintain her high position in a country that needed a very energetic hand at the helm. The Empress Wu encouraged Buddhism, admitting to her Court all those priests and monks who returned from India after years spent in study. And we know that she also encourageed the arts, since, apart from the support she gave to the Buddhist sculptors of Lung Men, to whom we shall return later, it was she who installed Yen Li-Pen, one of the greatest T'ang painters, in a high government position.

The T'ang poets and political thinkers, that brilliant coterie of which Tu Fu and Li Po formed the centre, flourished amidst the splendours of the reign of the Emperor Ming Huang (712–756), whose conception of the art of ruling consisted of prudently doing nothing at all. But idleness, however illuminated, has its disadvantages. The story of Yang Kuei-Fei has been painted, printed (on the printing presses invented just about that time) and recited for centuries. This Chinese Cleopatra inspired such passion in the breast of the Emperor that with the help of her groom, An Lu-Shan, she soon had him under her thumb. Though he was born a slave, Yang Kuei-Fei contrived to get An Lu-Shan appointed governor of a province and subsequently general commanding the Imperial Guard. A man of undoubted resource, he fomented a rebellion which was a first presage of the decline of the T'angs. For a hundred and fifty years after this first shedding of blood the dynasty managed to keep on its feet, living on the great achievements of its founders; it resisted continual pressure by barbarians on the frontiers and suppressed another revolt even bloodier than the first. As a result of this second revolt an official edict was published against the Buddhists, as the Confucian counsellors did not fail to take advantage of the opportunity to blame the new religion for all the evils which were afflicting China. In 845 the Emperor Wu Tsung ordered the destruction of all Buddhist monasteries and temples. It is impossible to estimate with accuracy the extent of the massacres which accompanied these acts of violence, but it is certain that by the time Hsüan Tsung, who succeeded the persecutor and last T'ang Emperor, revoked the edict, Buddhism had assumed a halo of martyrdom. The religion and its cult had been swept away, but the martyrs remained. It was a favourable moment for the advent of the moderate Ch'an sect, for its transformation and conquest—almost at the same time when one of the armies garrisoning the Annamite States revolted and marched on Ch'ang An.

After years of sanguinary civil war, the army at last reached the capital. Hsüan Tsung was obliged to vacate the throne. And thus perished the House of T'ang, the greatest and the most enlightened that the East has ever known.

*

The period immediately following on this glorious epoch is known as the FIVE DYNASTIES (A.D. 907–960), a name which is incorrect because thirteen Emperors belonging to eight families succeeded one another on the throne. It was another of those periods of transition constituting a crucible from which emerged the great Empire, transformed and enlightened by a new kind of genius. The imminent threat of the neighbouring nomads contributed towards the much-needed unity, since the Mongols were making those attempts at conquest which were one day to make them masters of half the then known world. General T'ai Tsu (960–976) and his son T'ai Tsung (976–997) were the great founders of the SUNG DYNASTY (A.D. 960–1279), which from the start turned its creative energy towards art. Buddhism, which had revived in the Ch'an form, found fertile ground. Disciplined introspection had restrained the ebullient T'angs, the spirit of military adventure had become the art of conservation and consolidation. The soldier was definitely replaced by the thinker. In reality, the State was weak, politically speaking, but the splendours of culture and art reached their highest point. A tranquil, serene felicity was the achievement of the time, a conquest which could only be achieved under a weak government, on the verge of disaster. In the meantime political ideologies were studied, and not only from the theoretical point of view. The philosopher-politician Wang An-Shih (1021–1086) realized that the lower classes must also be taken into consideration and studied the means of obtaining their support and putting them to the test. When we read his project today, it seems like a Communist Manifesto and nowadays Wang An-Shih is in fact considered in Peking to be

China's Karl Marx. The Mongols already represented a threat, but with Chu Hsi philosophy rose once more to those heights which it had reached in the golden age of Confucius.

All this was too good to last. The barbarian nomads were knocking ever more insistently at the gates. For the first time in China's history, and perhaps in the history of any nation, an army of more than a million men had to be raised. Wang An-Shih, who with the help of his theories had obtained the support of the populace, was in the end defeated by Court intrigues. Driven back by the Chin Tartars, who crossed the frozen Yellow River and occupied the capital, K'ai Feng, the Sungs withdrew to the south of the river and established themselves at Hangchow.

And here, surprisingly enough, after paying the necessary tribute to the Chins of the north, who became more and more independent and at the same time held back the barbarians now more barbarous than they were, the dynasty continued to prosper in the arts, in thought, and even in commerce, from 1127 to 1279. Under the exiled government the new capital became a brilliant intellectual centre, in which the spirit of China found its point of contact and exchange. The sanguinary and, on the whole, successful war waged by the Chins against the ferocious Genghis Khan induced the latter to seek better military fortune towards the west. But later his incredible successes gave him fresh courage and he again attacked China. In 1251, after defeating the Chin Emperor who had appealed in vain to the Sungs for help, Genghis Khan's mounted hordes swept into Southern China. Twenty-five years later, Genghis Khan's successor, Kublai Khan, entered the capital and mounted

the Celestial Throne, assuming on behalf of his family
the dynastic name of YUAN (1280–1368).

*

When we consider the elasticity shown by institutions based on Chinese ethics, even in face of a barbarian invasion, we realize the extent to which this
ethical system had penetrated the nation. Marco Polo
lived in China under the barbarian Yuan, yet his
descriptions show us a society flowering with civilization. After subjugating the Sungs, the conqueror
established his capital in Peking, the city of which Marco
Polo distorts the name from 'Khan Balik' (capital of
the Khans) to Cambaluc. The long war he had fought
on Chinese territory, and his previous experience gained
while overcoming the Chins, made it easy for the Yuan
emperor to adapt himself to Chinese ways of thinking
and methods. Kublai appreciated the advantages to be
gained from trade and encouraged it in every possible
way, especially by improving the means of communication; he also understood the emoluments that could
be derived out of culture and art and founded an
academy to which he summoned all the Sung scholars.
As for religion, he realized the restraining influence it
exercised on his subjects and protected all religions, in
particular Christianity, which he must have considered
the mildest of all, at all events judging from the New
Testament. He even invited emissaries to come to him
from Rome, but we know from Marco Polo that the
dangers of the journey frightened many, while in many
others ignorance of geography made any serious
attempt to get to China impossible. Nevertheless,

Giovanni da Montecorvino managed to reach China and build a church there—just as Buddhists, Taoists, Mohammedans and Jews continued to construct their places of worship. For his part the Emperor remained faithful to Chinese tradition and publicly supported Confucianism.

Unfortunately Kublai Khan had no worthy successors. After him, nine Emperors succeeded one another on the throne, thanks to Court intrigues in which the tenacious eunuchs played an important, if obscure, part. The last Yuan Emperor contrived to remain on the throne for thirty-five years, with the help of drastic measures to repress his subjects, whom religion did not seem to have tamed. The greatness of a tribe which conquers thanks to the intelligent exploitation of its horses is nullified, both in the East and in the West, when it comes up against real civilization. Shun Ti's measures represented a return to the brutal methods of his all-too-recent ancestors and caused his downfall. In fact he was driven back into the deserts of his forefathers by a Chinese monk turned soldier, another of the great men of China's history, who ascended the throne, assumed the name of Hung Wu and founded the great MING DYNASTY (1368–1644).

*

The best way of giving the reader a general idea of this period of Chinese history is to say that it greatly resembled the T'ang period. It was an age of great splendour and glory and one cannot help being astonished by the energy with which these men endeavoured to revive the glories of the past. And lastly we can admire the specimens of Chinese architecture in Peking, due to the Emperor Yung Lo, who courageously transferred his capital nearer to the battlefields, after Hung Wu had removed it to Nanking. The magnificence and beauty of these buildings, palaces and temples represent a return to the days of the T'angs; they are the oldest specimens of Chinese architecture extant, this being due to the fact that no buildings dating from before the Ming Dynasty have remained, wood and mortar being more ephemeral than stone. Like the T'angs, the Mings realized that passive defence is a negative conception and that the only real way of life is dynamic. The Emperor governed the country in accordance with the scheme outlined by the T'angs and by sending his armies to distant parts extended the frontiers of China still further. Trade and relations with foreign countries were further developed. Yung Lo ordered one of his eunuchs to supply him with information about countries as far away as Africa and even to get into contact with them. In a later chapter we shall see how these contacts were exploited in order to increase exports.

But after the death of Yung Lo in 1424, the dynamism which until then had given life to the country died away. In the static and complacent atmosphere of the palace the eunuchs could get busy again, and one of them, Liu Chin, became a real power in the land. The amount of treasures accumulated by him during his period of power would seem incredible to the younger generation of our own days, intent on eliminating even the conception of wealth.

Nonetheless this dynasty, too, ended quite serenely with the long reigns of Chia Ching (1522–1566) and Wan Li (1573–1619). Grave dangers were threatening from abroad; in addition to the barbarians in the north, the Japanese were becoming dangerous and Japanese pirates penetrated as far as Nanking. But such threats are the constant stimulant, the allopathic tonic that keeps a nation on the alert. If it succumbs, as the Ming Dynasty did in fact succumb to the Manchus, one ought to be able to assume that in time the country will eliminate the infection and return to new life.

The truth is that the total disintegration of this civilization which had endured for more than three thousand years was due to a deadly bacillus that gradually and silently worked its way into China. After being driven out together with the Mongols, together with their wares and their religious tracts, the Europeans were allowed to enter the country again and this time they established themselves firmly. Under the CHING DYNASTY (1644–1911), placed on the throne by the Manchus but absolutely Chinese in its methods, the Europeans living in China brought their relatives into the country and their appetites increased to such an extent that in the end they even summoned soldiers. When the Emperor Ch'ien Lung (1736–1795), not wishing to maintain contacts with such distant monarchs, told the British Ambassador to go home to his King, it was too late, though the Manchus did not realize this until another hundred years had elapsed.

In 1911 Sun Yat-Sen, the brother-in-law of Chiang Kai-Shek, contrived to overthrow the already toppling edifice, making use of slogans and a programme of appallingly ill-digested Western ideas. The Republic thus installed had less chance of succeeding than the democracy in a beehive, since the political training of the Chinese, this people who have made a religion of the past, has been that of a child as regards obedience and dependence—dependence on the patriarch in the family and on the Emperor in the nation. And only the following regime will know how to direct this ancient patriarchal conception towards a new patriarch—the State.

CHAPTER THREE

The Bronzes

THE beginnings of what is generally called ancestor-worship, of that Chinese first principle which, in the course of time, became an astute and very convenient ethical system, undoubtedly spring from that figure of the Cruel Father, so dear to modern psychologists, who carries on his despotic rule even after his death. The first time we encounter it, during the SHANG-YIN DYNASTY (?1766–1122? B.C.), it is already fully developed, so much so that the instruments necessary for its cult, made of a material that had only recently been discovered, namely bronze, seem to us, three thousand years later, the most beautiful examples of metal-casting the world has ever seen. And these bronzes prove that the Shang-Yins were the depositories of the oldest civilization of that time, always, of course, remembering that the milk of human kindness is a commodity of only recent invention and that for centuries mass human sacrifices were coupled with filial piety, artistic ability and religious organization.

Before we examine these ritual vases more closely, it will be better if we define the concept 'ancestor-worship', which might easily lead to erroneous interpretations. In actual fact, the Chinese did not worship their dead, but did everything possible to propitiate them. Once they had crossed the threshold separating life from death and were received into the mysterious silence inhabited by the Supreme Being, they possessed a certain power, even if this were only the influence they

PLATE 9. Mask of Tao-tieh in bronze. Early Chou Dynasty. Height 7¹/₂ inches (19 cm.). *Istituto del Medio ed Estremo Oriente, Rome.*

PLATE 10. Bronze *kuei*. Middle Chou Dynasty. Height 9 inches (23 cm.). *Freer Gallery of Art, Washington.*

PLATE 11. Bronze stag. From the Ordos Desert. Han Dynasty. Length 3½ inches (9 cm.). *Collection of Signora Cecilia Prodan, Rome.*

PLATE 12. Bronze back of a mirror. Late Chou Period. Diameter 5 inches (12.5 cm.). *Ostasiatiska Samlingarna, Stockholm.*

PLATE 13. White earthenware jar, unglazed. Shang-Yin Dynasty. Height 5 1/8 inches (13 cm.). *Freer Gallery of Art, Washington.*

PLATE 14. Figure in green glazed earthenware, with silvery iridescence. Han Dynasty. Height 7 1/2 inches (19 cm.). *Barling of Mount Street, Ltd., London*

could exercise on the gods. They were thus in a position to control the destinies of the living and it was therefore necessary to keep on good terms with them, by means of sacrifices and offerings of food and drink, and by gifts of the very instruments used for those rites, of the special utensils in which the food and drink—cereals, alcoholic beverages and wines produced from them—were prepared and preserved.

This ability to influence the fortunes of the family, which the Chinese have always attributed to their dead, is the effective basis of the ethical system of this practical race. Besides leading them to a rational acceptance of death as an inevitable spoke in a turning wheel, the other spokes of which are called birth, adolescence, maturity and old age, this belief encourages familiarity with the dead and makes it impossible for death to be considered as final. Moreover, as he becomes older, a man is more and more venerated because he is approaching the moment when he will become an ancestor; and old age thus becomes a synonym of virtue, because all know that at some future time they will possess this attribute. For their part, the old do all they can to deserve the prerogatives assigned to them. This is the most practical method of insuring against old age and guaranteeing good behaviour that has ever been excogitated and it also serves to inspire the whole family circle with lofty ethical principles.

*

The offerings for the propitiation of the dead and those for the worship of the gods were made in the appropriate place—by the rulers and the nobility in the ancestral temple, by the populace on the domestic hearth. The gods they worshipped were Shang Ti, the Supreme Being, and Shê, God of the Earth, second only to Shang Ti. Their altars were erected to the East and to the West, and since the pictograph of both was the phallic emblem, it is probable that they derive from very ancient fertility rites, precursors of those useful and agreeable rites that we mentioned in the preceding chapter.

But these were not the only gods worshipped by the primitive Chinese. Their pantheon was enriched by various minor deities: the gods of fire and of the wind, the spirits of the four cardinal points, the dragon-woman and many others. The King acted as mediator between them and the populace and the nobility. It was he who had to choose the most suitable method of maintaining harmonious relationship between heaven and earth, absolutely indispensable if one wanted to have a good harvest, many sons and military victories. The implements used by him for this purpose naturally had to be magnificent—and magnificent indeed are those brought to light in the course of the excavations near the royal residences in Anyang.

*

Whereas the Occidentals considered gold as a 'precious' metal, for the Chinese the most precious of all metals was an alloy of copper and tin. From the earliest times the skill of the bronze-workers reached a very high artistic level. The technical ability, developed in an era about which we are still completely in the dark, was such that by the first half of the second millennium B.C.

it had achieved sufficient mastery of the material to produce authentic works of art.

And here once again we encounter that Western presumption which crops up every time the archaeologists are faced with an enigma that subsequent excavations will almost certainly solve. Ignorance of the epochs preceding that of the Shang-Yins and the understandable reluctance to trust the classical Chinese legends (which attribute the invention of bronze-casting to a mythical Emperor Yü) have induced certain Western scholars to put forward the hypothesis that the technique of bronze-casting was imported into China from the West. And the unexpected discovery of such wealth of ability and technical knowledge, postulating a long period of study and evolution, does really seem to be an extraordinary enigma. A brief description of the method used in the casting of bronze will reveal how difficult it was and consequently how much skill was required of the artisan.

Although the modern Chinese learned about these magnificent bronzes from classical texts written before the sixth century, no description of the working methods has come down to us from these sources. We have therefore to rely on chemical analysis and a direct study of the objects in order to reach our conclusions. The metal is an alloy consisting of rather more than eight parts of copper to one part of tin and of negligible quantities of other metals. Some of the more primitive utensils must have been made by using moulds found on the site of the excavations, but for the most part the *cire perdue*, or lost wax, method was followed, whereby a solid core having the shape of the desired utensil was covered with a thin coating of wax, engraved, and then covered with very fine clay. Heat was then applied and the liquid wax escaped through holes made in the mud covering, leaving a perfect shell of hardened clay into which the molten bronze was then poured. As soon as the metal solidified, the clay covering was broken and a bronze utensil was obtained identical with the wax-covered model. It is certain that no artisan or goldsmith has ever equalled the skilful execution peculiar to the Chinese, let alone the architectonic originality of design or the power of the decorative motives. These objects have come down to us thanks to the veneration in which they were held and to the Shang belief in a future life, for which reason they buried them with their dead as gifts. This we know because many have been discovered in burial chambers, and also from inscriptions engraved on the utensils, clearly revealing the reason for their presence in the tombs. Nevertheless, the enormous interest aroused among scholars and collectors by these inscriptions, and the consequent great demand for them, resulted in the appearance in Peking, about 1930, of such skilful forgers that today all inscriptions must be viewed with a certain diffidence. In any case the scholars (presumably relying on authentic inscriptions) have been able to extract from them valuable information proving that even in the days of the Shang-Yins, the Chinese language possessed two thousand characters.

*

Whereas the shapes invented by the Chinese for these bronzes were sufficiently varied and numerous to constitute a presage of the genius peculiar to the race as regards the creation of forms, their morphology follows a scheme that might even be called gerarchical, a fixed order undoubtedly due to their ritual use. Each type has its name. To help the reader, we reproduce some of them below, confining ourselves to the simplest forms and, wherever possible, to the oldest, which served as models for the variations produced by subsequent periods.

The *ku* is, perhaps, among all these utensils, the most satisfying to our tastes. It was, obviously, a wine chalice with a concave support. Specimens exist with the most exquisite decorations ever found on bronzes. A similar type, the *tzun*, more squat and sturdy and sometimes square, was used for the same purpose.

The *chüeh* is another kind of cup used in the sacrificial consumption of wine. Although it may seem to have been derived from the *ting*, scholars think that the two vertical horns on the rim have a phallic origin and that this object must therefore be considered to be an elaboration of a very ancient form.

The *ho* was likewise used to contain wine, or else, since it has a spout and a lid, for mixing various alcoholic liquids by heating. The legs, bulb-shaped and concave, are a relic of the earliest clay form, the *li*, found also in bronze.

The *chih* is a rather small cup, sometimes provided with a lid. A similar form, with a larger body and a longer neck, is called *hu*, and must be held to be an elaboration of the *chih*, since it occurs more frequently in the Chou period than in the Shang-Yin. Another similar receptacle, though larger than the *chih* and almost always covered, is the *lei*.

Of all the receptacles for liquids the most impressive is the *yu*, since its creators exercised the greatest care in making it. No coarse examples of it exist and some have chased decorations worthy of the most famous modern goldsmiths. The *yu* occupies a place in the front rank in the gerarchy of bronzes, together with the *kuang*, a type of utensil that can be described as the reproduction of an animal in the form of a salt-cellar.

From the gastronomical point of view the most interesting container for food is the *hsien*, because it reveals the refinement of the *cuisine* still characteristic of the Chinese today. It was used for stewing meat; the lower portion, still retaining the prehistoric shape of the *lei*, contained water and was placed on the fire; the upper portion contained the food.

The *kuei* is another food-container. We reproduce it here in its simplest form, but other specimens exist with handles, and others with a square, concave base. They often have lids.

The *ting* is evidently derived from the pre-historic clay container with legs, which subsequently became the bronze *lei*. The two little projections on the rim were probably for carrying the container, by means of a pole inserted through them after heating.

The beautiful decorations make the *fang yi* the most magnificent of all food containers. It was probably used for keeping cereals intended for sacrificial purposes.

Ko knives and bronze hatchets similar to that shown on Plate 6 were likewise used for sacrificial purposes. Both these instruments often had delicate turquoise inlay work, revealing a surprisingly advanced technique.

The *cheng* here reproduced was probably the earliest form of bell. It was held upright and struck on the outside. Later it was turned upside-down and hung from a handle, which later became a hook. In that form it was called a *chung*.

That is a brief and restricted list of ritual utensils. Although there were not only subsequent derivatives from these forms, but also contemporary variations, the formal conception always remained intact, and was bound up with religious beliefs which in their essence are still mysterious to us today, even though we may talk glibly of Shê and the other gods. And the mystery becomes still deeper when we come to examine the marvellous decorations which consecrate these forms.

*

'Consecrate' is the right word. The animistic symbols, the spirals and scrolls (likewise symbolic) surrounding them and the formalism which governs them reveal an intention going far beyond a mere desire for decoration. And this, confirming, like the nobility of the shapes, the presence of something profound and reverent, transfers the artistic effort into another orbit. The grandeur of these bronzes lies precisely in this latent strength, in a majesty that can only spring from a very profound sentiment rather than from the need for embellishment. They possess the spirituality of men who created not for the sake of mundane glory, but for the sake of a transcendental glory. As in the chords of a *toccata* by Bach, in the bronze stem of a *tzun* we hear the ringing echoes of infinity. And in both, the stirring element is provided by the fact that their creators were listeners, consciously listening to the music of the galaxies, and not making vulgar attempts to be galaxies themselves. The impulse which drove them to create these bronzes was perhaps the first manifestation of the desire, peculiar to the Chinese, to be conciliatory spectators of the marvels of Nature, rather than protagonists.

In the decorations on these bronzes we find a further proof of what we have just said. Whereas the primitive Occidental sought to discover his magic in felicitous geometrical patterns, which at last explained everything, the Chinese bronzes with their complicated background of intertwining spirals which are neither round nor square, with the terrible animal masks that seem to be staring at us, enframed in tumultuous whirlpools like the waves of a stormy sea, the Shang-Yin bronzes contain nothing but questions, obscure and tremendous questions addressed to majestic gods. It would be wrong to suppose, however, that such decorations have only the sterile vitality of confusion. On the contrary, in the decorations, as in the forms, there is a potent formalism, a dominating conception, as deceptive as the square-round spirals forming the background, but which transform all vitality into tension and strength, like embankments restraining a tumultuous river.

As we have spoken of magic in connection with these decorations, it will be as well to explain what we mean by this rather vague term. The study of the exact meaning of the symbols adorning Shang-Yin bronzes has been rendered extremely difficult owing to the ignorance displayed by the Chinese texts—an ignorance expressed sometimes by silence and sometimes by quite unacceptable interpretations. Neverthless, the little we know about these decorations (from the study of the forms deriving from them and from simple induction) leads us to suppose that the magical element was based on a desire to obtain the favour of the gods by embellishing the utensils used in rites with symbols of what was asked of the gods.

The meaning of the omnipresent mask on Shang-Yin bronzes is still very obscure and the name *tao-tieh* given to such masks by Chinese scholars more than a thousand years later is even more deceptive than the silence in which they are shrouded. *Tao-tieh* means 'glutton'. The mental effort which this name has imposed upon

Chinese scholars of later periods and on Western investigators has resulted in most unexpected conclusions. The most recent interpretation of these monstrous faces is that they represent, in a stylized form, the mask of a tiger. From inscriptions engraved on oracle-bones and confirmed by the Chinese classics, we know that from the earliest times the tiger had some connection with the earth, which was worshipped more than any other divinity during the Shang-Yin period. In addition to this, the habitat of the tiger was towards the west, and the altars dedicated to Shê, goddess of the earth, faced towards the west. The fact that the masks on these bronzes often have features which are not those of the tiger, may be due to other forms of symbolism. The diamond-shaped lozenge often seen on their foreheads is a symbol of fertility, the vulva, while the vertical horns with flattened ends could be interpreted as phallic symbols. It is interesting to note that, whereas the representation of the genital organs played an important role in the religions of advanced civilizations such as the Greek and the Roman, during the Shang-Yin period it was already a secondary element, destined to disappear definitely at the beginning of the first millennium B.C. (Plate 9).

On the other hand we can make use of Chinese texts when we come to consider the multiform aspects of the dragon, a mythical Chinese animal which here makes its first appearance. Although representing heaven, which is its abode, the dragon is also the counterpart and at the same time the complement of earth. From the harmony between the two comes fertility. On the oracle-bones the dragon is mentioned as a propitious symbol of celestial benevolence. Later it became the emblem of the Emperor and in fact the texts tell us that

74

the first Son of Heaven was the result of intercourse between his mother and a dragon. Its altar faced towards the east, the cardinal point of heaven.

Other stylized animals appear on the bronzes, but before examining them we must consider the spirals filling the background. We have already mentioned the great vitality these spirals give to the whole decorative motive. They represent lightning, thunder and rain. It is difficult to imagine a more successful representation of these potent forces of Nature, a representation which made its first appearance on the prehistoric earthenware of which we shall speak in the next chapter.

Two other stylized animals often found on Shang-Yin bronzes as background motives are the cicada and the snake. After reasoned, but somewhat complicated, deductions it has been assumed that they respectively represent the harvest and water. Shells are also often found, likewise symbols of fertility owing to their resemblance to the female genital organ, and this despite the fact that under the Shangs shells were used as coins. In fact some scholars hint at the possibility that such representations on bronzes could be interpreted as prayers for wealth.

Another animal which sometimes plays as important a role as the *tao-tieh* is the owl, symbol of night, darkness and the feminine forces of Nature. In this eternal struggle between Yin and Yang, between the male and female elements which counteract and at the same time complete each other, the pheasant is the male symbol, the emblem of the sun. And as such it was dear to the Empress, whose symbol it eventually became after being transformed into a phoenix.

In the Shang-Yin bronzes the elephant is used as a

symbol of fertility, as it was for thousands of years in other Eastern countries.

The reader will perhaps have noticed that among the gods who were propitiated in the hope of receiving favours we have not yet mentioned the Supreme Being, Shang Ti. The oracle-bones give to this deity a form embodying certain human attributes. He is the only divinity so treated and we may therefore conclude that the only anthropomorphic symbol found on these bronzes is a representation of Shang Ti himself. Nevertheless, it is rarely found, the lid of a *ho* in the Freer Art Gallery (Plate 4) being one of the very few specimens that have come down to us. The phallic horns of the god express an incitement to fertility, while his human aspect shows that he is the great ancestor of the whole human race. The sacred vessels on which he is represented, together with other minor divine symbols, constitute the highest invocation of the Supreme Being. A lady scientist has put forward the hypothesis that the scarcity of representations of this male god on ritual bronzes might be attributable to the fact that, in China as in other Asiatic-Occidental civilizations, priestesses were usually preferred to priests, and the former naturally gave preference to female divinities. This is really a very interesting supposition.

*

The historical vicissitudes so inadequately narrated in the preceding chapter should still be sufficiently fresh in the conscientious reader's mind to enable him to recall the tranquil, one might almost say courteous, conquest of the country by the feudal CHOU DYNASTY

(?1122–221 B.C.). The stylistic transition in the bronzes from one period to the other is equally smooth and gentle. Professor Bernhard Karlgren, the most assiduous labourer in this insidious vineyard, is continually putting forward new and different theories affecting the historical dates we have given. The Yin of the name Shang-Yin, for example, is a new addition due to this eminent Swedish scholar, an addition not yet accepted by his American colleagues, even though he claims to have discovered that the Shangs were subsequently called Yin. Nevertheless, it is to Professor Karlgren that we owe an explanation far more plausible than the traditional Chinese theory according to which style changed brusquely and often radically on the fall of a dynasty or, in more recent times, on the death of an Emperor. According to Professor Karlgren, style remained unchanged during the whole of the *Early Chou Period*, that is to say until 900 B.C., and the artisan-casters merely went on producing faithful copies of the magnificent Shang-Yin works. As is always the case when it is a matter of copies, inferior inspiration should be discernible and it is in fact on the basis of this very problematic criterion that we are able to identify the products of this period.

The products of the *Middle Chou Period* (about 900–600 B.C.), on the other hand, are easily recognizable—always assuming that no new theories are evolved implying another transposition of the historical data. But in any case this could only affect the historical background, since the derivation of this group of products from the previous one is in many respects obvious, especially in one particular respect. The products of this group no longer reveal the intense religious feeling

77

of the Shang-Yin bronzes. The utensils and their surface embellishments have become pure and simple decoration—a decoration due more to the effect they produce than to real beauty. The *kuei* is placed on a pedestal and remains there, while the most beautiful Shang-Yin types—the *ku*, the *tzun*, the *chüeh* and the *yi*—gradually disappear. The background spirals symbolizing the elements of Nature become rarer and the stylized cicadas and pheasants are replaced by rather obtuse-looking elephants, forming a utensil of a new kind. The *cheng* is now definitely transformed into the *chung* which, turned upside down, flourishes lustily during this and the following period. The truth is that the Chinese artisan has lost his religion. A new era is ushered in. The days of the great philosophers are coming and the spiritual void will soon be filled by Lao Tzu, Confucius and Mo Tzu.

*

It is at this point that we find ourselves face to face with a style which, in many respects, is comparable in its beauty and intensity with the magnificent Shang-Yin bronzes. The historical denomination of these products has undergone many vicissitudes. Starting with 'Ch'in' (at a time when all Shang-Yin works were still called 'Chou' owing to an excessive Western mistrust of the Chinese texts), and passing through 'Warring States' (because at the end of the Chou period the States were at war) and later 'Huai' (from the valley in which the first specimens of this style were found), we have now reached the denomination *Late Chou Period* (about 600–256 B.C.), and for that we have once more to thank Professor Karlgren.

The salient characteristic of this style is its vitality. The Shang animals, volutes and spirals which now re-appear are again in movement. And in the midst of this notable dynamism, realistic renderings of animals and even of human beings suddenly appear for the first time. From this period date the first sculptures in bronze. And towards the beginning of the period, in the distant Gobi, the Ordos, a nomad civilization, cast in bronze magnificent animals and splendid medallions with animistic compositions, many of them revealing strong Shang influence. We know little else about the Ordos, though hypotheses have been advanced connecting them with the Scyths (Plate 11).

In China itself the human form was more and more used, together with those of animals, in various positions and in movement. This was an evolution dating from the times when such realistic representations, though far more rigid, served as supports for the utensils. Animals of noteworthy vigour were carved to make hooks for the *chung*, or bell, now embellished with strange protuberances. In a certain sense, these animals were the synthesis of all the late Chou style.

The large-scale use of inlay on stone and metals was introduced. Compositions in gold, silver and turquoise, of excellent taste and beauty, were used to adorn finials and trappings, especially towards the end of the period.

But the definite vulgarization of the material becomes evident when we consider the enormous production of bronze mirrors at this time. The metal, hitherto used for the edification of the spirit, now enters the boudoirs of ladies and there could be no clearer evidence of the important role played by women in those civilized times than the backs of these mirrors. Apart from their refinement and elegance, the decorations are exquisite geometrical drawings, executed with the greatest care. Even greater care was perhaps given to another article of profane use, the so-called belt-hook worn on the shoulder to fasten the upper fold of the garment. The finest specimens of these have exquisite inlays and some of them even whole pieces of real jade.

*

This production continued during the short CH'IN DYNASTY (221-206 B.C.) until it flowed into the great HAN DYNASTY (206 B.C.–A.D. 220). The animal forms gradually disappeared and simplicity became the pass-word as far as utensils were concerned. The *tao-tieh* becomes merely a decorative motive designed to conceal the ringed hook. But on the smooth and elegant surfaces the fascinating patina of time finds no obstacle to its flow.

Carved animals become simpler in form, with success-ful attempts to render movement. Mirrors became more and more numerous and remained popular until the T'ang Dynasty. But the era of the bronzes is now drawing to a close and no more interest is taken in the material. The little gilded bronzes from the Wei and T'ang Dynasties are really magnificent carvings in which the choice of material is only incidental (Plate 32).

Neverthless, it was in bronze that the Chinese ex-pressed their basic conception of form, perhaps more through Han simplicity than in the golden age of this metal. And it is from the bronzes that the potters will take their subjects, which they will develop intelligently, to produce on their wheels variations constituting the greatest museum in the world for the lovers of form.

PLATE 15. Camel in red earthenware, unglazed. Wei or Sui Dynasty. Length 9 inches (23 cm.). *Collection of Avvocato Umberto Ortolani, Rome.*

PLATE 16. Horse in white earthenware, unglazed. T'ang Dynasty. Height 26³/₄ inches (
Collection of Dott. Alessandro Campilli, Rome.

PLATE 17. Polo-player in red earthenware, unglazed. T'ang Dynasty.
Length 12¼ inches (31 cm.). *Private collection.*

PLATE 18. Female dancer in white earthenware, unglazed. T'ang Dynasty.
Height 8 5/8 inches (22 cm.). *Barling of Mount Street, Ltd., London.*

CHAPTER FOUR

Earthenware and Porcelain

Iт is thanks to religion that the moulding of clay became an art among the Chinese long before, and to a much greater extent, than was the case among the other peoples of antiquity. From the moment it was discovered, earthenware became the expression of ancestor-worship. The utensil—originating from the divine element 'earth', from which it suddenly took shape with the aid of another divine element, fire—even if it were only intended for household purposes, was surrounded by the same aura of spirituality as the domestic hearth. It is also quite possible that the discovery of metals was due to the potters, as a result of the firing of clays containing metals. It is therefore not illogical to suppose that such miracles endowed this art with a very special importance. The objects themselves, which have come down to us from tombs in a continuous stream, show better than any other evidence all the diligence, inventiveness and artistic training that must have constituted the heritage of this category of artisans and of every one of its members. We shall see how the story of the potter's art was one of conquests and discoveries which, considered in relation to the basic concepts of Chinese life, are as surprising as those of the inventors of our modern scientific world. But the diversity of intent and system was enormous. Here we do not find academic revelations for the welfare of mankind, but a formula kept jealously secret and never entrusted to writing, established empirically by means of tests made in the palm of the hand, possible only because of a profound and intimate sense of touch—a formula based on the senses which was handed down from father to son from one generation to another. Shining with that truth which the Taoist doctrine borrowed from the flux and reflux of Nature, we see the robust colours created by the ancestors become inexorably paler and paler, a pitiless revelation of the weakening stamina of their successors. Everything is personal. Every success and every experiment are family property, even when definite requirements made a reluctant acceptance of organization inevitable. One may well say that in no other part of the world was Candide's discovery more obvious than here; in no other country more than in China did the individual turn his back on his neighbours and till his own garden.

*

How is it possible to discover a method, a system, enabling us to establish definitely the degree of beauty possessed by an object? A rigid classification based on a formula of the beauty of natural things would certainly show the absurdity of such a pretension. Our faculty of appreciation is very elusive, and, like all our other faculties, liable to be influenced by education and by a certain training which will allow it to look beyond the fashion of the moment and establish a kind of common denominator. It is this faculty which enables us to regard as art the skill of the Chinese potter and it is in deference to it that we shall make no further comment on the various pieces presented here, leaving each of them to proclaim its own beauty through its appearance alone. And it was this same faculty, in this case not contemplative but active, that inspired the potter as he worked the shapeless clay on his wheel. Yes, the choice of the shape was really dictated by this faculty, though naturally not by it alone. There were requirements other than aesthetic, and some knowledge of the problems of raw material and purpose the potter had to face will probably throw light on the importance of this faculty of beauty which inspired the hands of the artisan. Apart from the presentation of the photographs, the aim of this chapter will therefore be to examine such problems and the classification of the various pieces not only according to their chronology, but also according to their geographical origins, for in the classification of works in earthenware, more than in that of any other branch of art, the Chinese attach quite as much, if not more, importance to the place of origin as they do to the historical date.

*

In the preceding chapter we have already mentioned the Yang Shao and Lung Shan earthenware of the pre-historic age. We can thus begin here by saying what we know about the earthenware of the SHANG-YIN DYNASTY (?1766–1122? B.C.). We at once come across the proof that, at least from the earliest historic periods, the potter worked to honour his ancestors. Even though now reduced to fragments, all the objects found in the Shang areas in Northern Honan remind us of the shapes of the ritual bronze utensils. Here we have another confirmation of a hypothesis we have already put forward: does the fine white paste of these fragments contain kaolin? And if so, in what quantity? How great a degree of heat could it stand and to what degree of heat was it actually subjected? And if there is no answer to any of these questions, how can we be certain that we are really dealing with porcelain? How can we affirm that the supporters of this hypothesis are wrong and that consequently porcelain which, according to evidence preceding the Shang excavations, was first produced in China about the tenth century A.D. (and in Medicean Florence about 1580), was not in reality being produced in Honan about 2500 years before? One of the very few items of news we have received from Communist China mentions another type of paste, also found in the Shang area, in the province of Shensi. It is 'a hard and thin earthenware with umber-coloured glaze, which might be the ancestor of Chinese porcelain and perhaps of all the glazed earthenware in the world'. It is true, as this article in *China Reconstructs* goes on to say, that before these discoveries, it was believed that glazes were used for the first time on earthenware during the Han Dynasty, that is to say about a thousand years later.

All this may seem to some of our readers extremely meticulous, or even an attempt to exaggerate the importance of a factor in itself irrelevant, since glazed earthenware is very similar to porcelain and equally fragile. We must therefore make it clear that porcelain requires so much skill and experience and such a quantity of empirical research-work that a nation which masters such a complicated technique, and achieves artistic excellence by this means, must perforce have a higher level of culture than that required for making and decorating ordinary earthenware.

The knowledge of the making of porcelain is generally

somewhat limited; it is felt, therefore, that it may help even the cultured reader if we give a simple explanation of the technique required, an explanation which will also serve to clarify the difference between earthenware, *grès* and porcelain.

These three materials are all derived from clay—composed of aluminium silicate and varying quantities of silica and other materials—which achieves a certain degree of hardness in accordance with the temperature at which it is fired: over 800°C. in the case of earthenware and as much as 1450°C. in the case of certain types of very hard European porcelain. Earthenware remains porous because it can only stand a low degree of heat. In order to increase the temperature to the melting-point of clay and at the same time avoid breaking the utensil, it is necessary to add, or to increase the existing quantity of, certain ingredients, namely silica in various forms (sand, powdered quartz, or ground potsherds). On exposure to a high degree of heat, this mixture melts and the resulting material, as impermeable as stone, is called *grès*. This gives us the so-called 'body' of the utensil, usually brown in colour, since the action of fire on the commonest clays changes the original colour, which is due to the presence of iron. Common white clays, that is to say those which remain white even after exposure to heat, are not malleable enough to be wrought on the wheel. They are therefore used for painting, for giving a different colour to the brown 'body', and this covering is known technically as the 'slip', because usually another more elaborate coating covers the 'body' above the 'slip'. By this we mean the glaze, often as transparent as a woman's dress so as to allow the 'slip' to give colour to the whole figure.

This glaze, resembling glass, is applied to earthenware mainly to make it impermeable, whereas in the case of *grès* and porcelain, which are already impermeable, it is merely an embellishment.

The glazes are made in a way very similar to that followed in making glass, i.e. of silica to which are added lime, potash or a lead oxide. One special type, however, is derived from fusible stone, and this is the Chinese potter's own contribution to the technique. We know nothing about how it was made, and perhaps for this reason the glaze on the Anyang fragments has always been an enigma for technical experts.

Porcelain, on the other hand, is composed of a highly refractory clay that remains white even after firing and which the Chinese call kaolin. When it is mixed with *petuntze*, more fusible than kaolin, it can stand up to 1300°C. of heat. Both these materials consist of decomposed stone, though this is less true of the former than of the latter. The function of the *petuntze* is to hold together the particles of kaolin, which remains obstinately solid when exposed to heat. It is for this reason that the Chinese consider kaolin to be the bones of porcelain and *petuntze* the flesh.

Such then was the great invention of the Chinese—the idea of using powdered stone for making utensils instead of earth alone. This, however—though the simplest inventions are often the greatest—would contrast with what we have already said about the complicated technique of porcelain production, were it not for the fact that a corollary of this discovery was the intricate, even though empirical, study of the exact doses required, and to an even greater extent, the ability to build ovens and kilns for melting down the rock. It is sufficient to mention that it was the inability to produce such a temperature that prevented the Europeans from repeating the achievements of the Medicean potters, until 1710, when Johann Friedrich Böttger built a factory at Meissen which was destined to find a definite solution of the problem.

*

A brief description of the preliminary work needed in order to make the raw material fit for use will perhaps give an idea of the difficulties the potter had to overcome. Even during the period we were discussing when we plunged into this technical digression clay was being extracted from the soil at Tzuchow, twelve miles from the Shang capital, where quarries and kilns are still functioning today. It was then conveyed to the factories and left for a long time in the open air, exposed to the weather which broke it up and softened it. One of the very few references to Chinese art in Marco Polo's story of his journey tells us how he saw enormous piles of this material and examined some of the articles made from it. Here are his words: 'I will also tell you that in this province, in a city called Tiunjiu, they make plates of porcelain in all sizes and among the most beautiful that can be imagined. They are a speciality of this city and from here are sent to all parts of the world. They are produced in great quantity and at a low price, so low, in fact, that with a Venetian groat one could purchase three of the most beautiful. These plates are made of mud, as I will explain. You must know then that the men of the said city collect a mud composed of decayed earth, make great piles of it and leave it there for thirty or forty years, exposed to the wind, the sun and the rain, never touching the piles during all this time. In this way the piles of earth are purified to such a point that the plates made from it have a bluish colour and are very brilliant and of extraordinary beauty. They are painted in the colours desired and baked in a furnace. You must know that when a man makes a pile of this earth, he does it for his sons, because, owing to the very long time required for its preparation, no man can hope to gain any personal profit or to use it himself. The fruits will go to the son who comes after him.' Marco Polo wrote those words in the fourteenth century, but the usage was far older and has probably remained unchanged for three thousand years. The stone was ground to a very fine powder in mills and then suspended in water to enable the finest particles to separate from the coarser grains. This process was repeated several times and finally the clay, now very fine indeed, was allowed to harden until it formed a ductile and perfect paste.

The next stage was to reduce the paste to long sausage-shaped strips, twisting it in such a way that it took on the form of a utensil, after which it was smoothed so as to give a uniform surface, both outside and inside. As we have already seen, potter's wheels were being used about 3000 B.C.; these wheels consisted of discs rotating horizontally, the clay being placed in the centre. When the wheel was rotated, centrifugal force made the clay spread. The hand of the potter controlled and directed this force: he would raise the clay, thus permitting it to spread and then contract again, or he would bend it to his will, just as the hand of a musician creates a form of sound on the keyboard of a piano.

PLATE 19. Porcelain jar, Shin-Yao type. T'ang Dynasty. Height
7 1/2 inches (19 cm.). *Collection of Dott. Alessandro Campilli, Rome.*

PLATE 20. Vase in porcellaneous stoneware with ivory-coloured glaze. Tzu-chou type.
Sung Dynasty. Height 15³/₄ inches (40 cm.). *Freer Gallery of Art, Washington.*

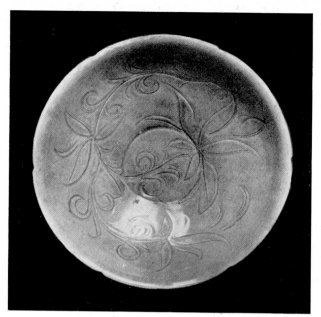

PLATE 21. Bowl in porcellaneous stoneware. *Ting-yao*. Sung Dynasty. Diameter 7 7/8 inches (20 cm.). *Museum für Ostasiatische Kunst, Cologne*.

PLATE 22. Bowl in porcellaneous stoneware. *Lung-chuan yao*. Diameter 6 3/4 inches (17 cm.). *J. Nowell Collection, London*.

PLATE 23. Vase in white porcelain. *Shu fu.* Yuan Dynasty. Height 13³/₄ inches (34 cm.). *Collection of His Excellency Alexandre J. Argyropoulos, Athens.*

PLATE 24. Jug in white porcelain. *Blanc de Chine*. Ming Dynasty. *Collection of Avvocato Umberto Ortolani, Rome.*

PLATE 25. Box in white porcelain. Ming Dynasty, Yung Lo period. Diameter 6³/₄ inch (17.5 cm.). *Collection of Marchese G. Litta-Modignani, Capalbio.*

PLATE 26. Porcelain bowl. Green on yellow glaze. Ming Dynasty. Height $4^1/_8$ inches (10.5 cm.). *Collection of Marchese G. Litta-Modignani, Capalbio.*

PLATE 27. Porcelain bowl. Chia-Ching mark. Diameter $7^1/_2$ inches (19 cm.).
The Percival David Foundation, London.

This was the moment of intimacy between the potter, his clay and the live rotating wheel, a moment of concentration made up of space, time and vision, and of concentration on the use to which the utensil would be put. For the beauty of a Chinese vase is inseparable from its functional purpose, like the creations of modern architects. None of the instruments used by modern potters to help them to obtain the form desired was used by the Chinese potter, who, although he used moulds for certain mass-produced articles, preferred to fashion all the finer pieces separately. After the clay had been hardened by exposure to air the utensils were put back on the wheel and finished off with a paring knife, in order to make certain parts thinner and to carve out the base, which previously had remained attached to the wheel.

After being dried, the body of the utensil was ready to be decorated—by means of engraving, pressure or the application of plastic elements such as, for example, the masks of animals carrying rings in their mouths which were used as handles. After the application of the 'slip', they were further decorated by painting on the surface. In this last field, and especially in the case of the daring Sung creations, the Chinese potter had no equal. We find here the vital impulse and spirit peculiar to Chinese written characters. It often seems as if the rendering of Nature has been forced in order to give it more power, or as if, after passing through a human sieve, Nature takes on a form more easily conceivable by mankind. (Oscar Wilde, rashly presumptuous, considered Nature to be an 'imitation' of art, because it made a less forcible impression on him than the distillate of Nature produced by his artist friends.)

This Chinese power is particularly noticeable when the potter painted underneath the glaze. When, however, he painted on top of the coating of glaze (enamel painting), the meticulousness inherent in the required technique limited his audacity. It would, however, be wrong to attribute to this factor the degeneration from 'beautiful' to merely 'pretty' of the pieces produced during the last period; in art, the 'pretty' is a symptom of decadence, not a diversion.

But let us return once more to our utensil, which has now been covered with its 'slip' and dried again. There are three methods of applying glaze: the article can be immersed in a liquid (water) in which powdered minerals are in suspension, or the glaze can be applied with a brush or blown on by using a tube to the extremity of which a piece of gauze has been attached to serve as an atomizer.

Only after this is the utensil subjected, once and for all, to the 'great fire', this being contrary to Western practice, according to which it is fired for the first time when still bare, until the 'biscuiting' has been completed, then glazed and then returned to the kiln. The Chinese method is more risky, but the resulting product is more genuine: frequently the glaze fuses with the kindred elements in the utensil to such an extent that it becomes an integral part of it, so that, when we examine shards, it is impossible to say where the body ends and the glaze begins.

The colouring of the glazes was obtained by using oxides of copper, iron, cobalt and manganese and by regulating the influx of air into the furnace so as to cause oxidization. Copper gave a fine range of reds, while iron produced magnificent yellows, browns and blacks when the furnace was full of air, and the grey-green nuances of celadon when the amount of air was reduced and smoke and carbon monoxide were formed. Faithful to its nature, cobalt produced various shades of blue, whatever the amount of oxygen present, while manganese gave the beautiful peacock blue, violet and purple.

For us it is easy to talk of oxygen, of oxides and monoxides—abstruse terms of which we gained a superficial knowledge during chemistry lessons at school. But we must remember that the Chinese were devoid of the most elementary scientific notions, that a furnace emitting smoke might be the prelude to a disaster, and that, sooner or later, every type of mineral was brought into contact with fire. Only if we remember this can we gain an insight into the long and patient series of futile experiments that had to be made before a working knowledge of the complete process could be at last acquired. Anyway, we may be grateful to the scientific ignorance of the Chinese for giving us rich and magnificent glazes, even if they are imperfect from the chemical point of view. Nowadays science, after eliminating all impurities, bubbles and the tendency to crack which is a feature of old Chinese glazes, offers us others having all the perfection of a good-quality window-pane.

*

Let us now return to the history of our subject by telling the reader of certain very interesting discoveries made recently in the islands surrounding the British colony of Hong Kong. Thanks mainly to the work of

Western amateurs, there have come to light utensils made of a hard, glazed material that could rightly be described as *grès*. Although it is impossible to date them with accuracy, British scholars are inclined to ascribe them to the CHOU DYNASTY (?1122–221 B.C.), to which is also attributed a grey pottery, unglazed, copying all the forms of bronzes, found near Loyang and in the province of Shantung. A recently discovered hatchet is interesting. Whereas all the pottery with decorations derived from the bronzes hitherto found in these areas consists of utensils (to such an extent that it has been difficult to decide whether the forms of the bronzes derive from those of the pottery or *vice versa*), this article, absolutely unsuitable for any practical purpose, shows that the pottery found in the area was intended to replace the valuable ceremonial articles in metal, probably so that they might accompany mortals of minor importance to the next world.

To the end of this period many scholars also attribute a whole series of very interesting objects in earthenware, presumably found at Hui-hsien in Northern Honan. The surface of these objects, often lacquered, is of a brilliant smooth black, with certain portions painted with a magnificent red and cyclamen-coloured pigment. A violent controversy is now raging between the scholars whose institutions have been able to acquire some of these objects and those who have been unable to do so. The former assert, and quite logically, that if the objects in question are really forgeries, as the latter maintain, then the man who produced the whole series must have been a Picasso or even Epstein himself, which would be rather unlikely in the China of those days. The incredulous, on the other hand, maintain that the style of the figures does not in any way follow the evolution of Chinese figurative representation and that many pieces having exactly the same material characteristics as the finest pieces are obvious and clumsy forgeries. These experts refuse to consider that the late Chou period was one of revolutionary artistic innovation and that, on the other hand, the technical problems of imitation are much easier to solve than the artistic ones.

It was during the HAN DYNASTY (206 B.C.–A.D. 220) that the potter's art made those great strides which were to lead to a multiform development in Chinese ceramics. As always, we owe all our direct knowledge of the products of this period to the activities of tomb-robbers in Honan, Shansi and Shensi, and it is therefore impossible to discover the exact provenance of the various types—an impossibility which we shall have to accept down to the Ming Dynasty. The forms of the utensils are surprisingly reminiscent of the Roman simplicity of the Republican period. The body, rarely grey or white, is often burnt to a brick red, but it is the glaze that constitutes the great novelty of this period, a magnificent hyaline coating obtained by the use of lead silicate. The colour is green (copper oxide) or, more rarely, yellowish brown. The green glaze in particular, when it comes into contact with the minerals in the earth, acquires a beautiful gold and silver iridescence which gives a strange delicacy to the surface of the pottery, in itself simple or even coarse (Plate 14).

The objects that have come down to us were evidently intended for the dead. They are containers for cereals and wine, replicas of domestic utensils and farm animals, complete with stables. Human figures seldom occur. One type of receptacle is decorated with horizontal bands on the upper portion of the body representing hunting scenes, while handles and ring imitate the bronze prototypes. These scenes are somewhat disconcerting: the figures of horses and horsemen are in marked contrast to the somewhat primitive style of the domestic animals made at that time and reveal a close affinity with the bronze medallions from the Ordos desert. But this diversity might be attributed not so much to evolution as to the locality where the pieces were found, which we do not know because of the confusion deliberately caused by the robbers of tombs in order to conceal the place of their misdeeds. Here, too, Western scholars have reached the conclusion that not only are the glaze and form of these receptacles of Hellenic-Iranian inspiration, but also that they must be attributed to the end of the Han Dynasty, since lead oxide glazes were not used in the West until 100 B.C. Nevertheless, it is difficult to see how these hypotheses can stand after the recent discoveries proving that Chinese potters knew about glazes more than a thousand years before that time.

It was at this time that the production began of those glazed earthenware tiles, destined to continue for centuries down to our own times. And to the Han Dynasty is likewise attributed that unglazed grey pottery with decorations *à froid* in white and red of great vivacity and elegance. Unfortunately this type of ceramic generally reaches us in fragments and we must mention that the date attributed to it is anything but certain because the style of the geometrical drawings reminds us of a later period.

*

Lastly, the invention of porcelain is attributed to the Chinese, during the period of the SIX DYNASTIES (A.D. 220–589), but owing to a philological controversy as to the exact meaning of the term 'porcelain', scholars have christened it 'proto-porcelain' or 'porcellaneous stoneware'. The Chinese word *tzu* denotes a type of glazed ceramics so hard that they cannot be scratched with a knife and which emit a ringing sound when struck. Our term 'porcelain', on the other hand, stipulates that, in addition to having those characteristics, the material must also be white and translucent. The pieces in question, found in Fukien, Shensi, Kiangsu and Korea, have very hard, grey bodies containing kaolin, covered first with a reddish or light grey 'slip' and then with an olive-brown glaze, which, in most cases, adorns only the upper portion of the utensil, producing original and extremely daring effects. As a type, it is very similar to the Yüeh ceramics of which we shall speak later and the forms still re-echo those of the bronzes of the Han period (to which some modern Chinese scholars would like to attribute them). It is impossible to discover with certainty where they come from, but it is thought that they may have been made in the kilns at Yüeh-chow in Chekiang, which continued operating until the Ming period.

To the SUI DYNASTY (A.D. 589–618) are attributed certain delicate white figurines, covered with a slightly iridescent, lead oxide glaze and often painted in magnificent blues and reds. Another type of pottery, greyish and with 'slips' generally of a reddish-brown colour, is attributed to the Wei period of the preceding Six Dynasties, for reasons of style, though it should, more correctly, be assigned to the Sui Dynasty.

Here the Bactrian camel makes its first appearance, together with noble horses (with trappings like our tournament horses in the Middle Ages), bulls and men fully equipped for war, with finely incised features, robust and delicate at the same time (Plate 15).

*

But these figures and animals are merely the heralds of that vast production of funerary pottery that flourished throughout the Empire during the T'ANG DYNASTY (A.D. 618–906). We must here keep our promise to study the efforts made by Chinese artists to honour their dead, noting first of all the plastic ability of the potters who contrived to give such life and dignity to products made on such a vast scale. We have to turn to Greek or Etruscan art to find a counterpart to the proud nobility of T'ang earthenware horses, to the subtle grace and simple elegance of the maidens made of a soft, white and pink clay. Nor must we fail to stress the enormous diffusion of this artistic talent. Chinese sources speak of as many as seventeen provincial production centres (Chihli, Chekiang, Kiangsi, Honan, etc.), but those who have never seen with their own eyes the great quantities of funerary sculptures coming from the tombs at Loyang alone, are bound to regard with a certain mistrust the very large number of pieces that have come to light (Plates 16, 17, 18).

While there are some very fine specimens without any hyaline covering, most of them are embellished with rich and magnificent glazes in five colours—white, yellow, green, brown, and a beautiful and very rare indigo blue—usually combined together, but also used by itself. The utensils have a noble simplicity forecasting the forms of Sung porcelain. Some of the plates show engraved or pressed decorations filled with colour: flowers, animals stylized to conform with the technique used, not unlike those on the Fa Hua porcelain we shall discuss later (Plate B).

Really porcellaneous, on the other hand, are the wonderful white and ivory-coloured pieces now shamelessly described as 'T'ang porcelain'. Some specimens fulfil all European requirements, being thin and translucent, while others, though always white and hard, have slightly fatter bodies, not, however, devoid of a sober and robust beauty. There are dishes, boxes for face-powder and cosmetics, mugs and vases, some of them shaped like a Greek amphora, with handles consisting of curved dragons biting the orifice of the elongated neck and adhering tightly to the body. This is a familiar form found down to the Ming period, though it is also found on the glazed pottery of the T'ang Dynasty.

*

The connecting link between the glazed pottery of the Six Dynasties, the first official appearance of what we choose to call 'proto-porcelain', and the beautiful 'Celadon' pieces of the Sungs and the Mings, is the now famous and popular Yüeh-yao (*yao* means kiln), very similar to the former in body and glaze, but differing in shape and decoration. These pieces are obvious precursors of the later Ming styles, especially as regards the utensils for ordinary use, whereas the utensils shaped like animals have a plastic strength reminiscent of T'ang pottery and Wei sculpture in stone. All these products are attributed to the FIVE DYNASTIES (A.D. 907–960), one reason being that Chinese texts speak of two famous ceramics of the period: Ch'ai-yao (really fabulous because we know nothing absolutely about it) and Yüeh-yao, and maintain that both were destined for Emperors, or at all events for princes. This porcellaneous stoneware was produced in kilns lying about forty miles to the east of that same city Yüeh-chow from which it is supposed that most of the proto-porcelain of the Six Dynasties came. It should be noted that a large number of pieces of this type have come to light in comparatively recent times and that, while some of them are of very fine quality, others are so coarse as to render doubtful the statements in the Chinese texts that they were exclusively reserved for Court use. Another peculiar circumstance is that this type of ceramics, so obviously deriving from that of the sixth century, remained unknown during all the three hundred years of T'ang rule. From that one might deduce that although our recourse to Chinese sources is justified by the inadequacy of our direct archaeological knowledge, it would be advisable to be rather elastic in our assertions regarding dates, in order to create the connecting link between these two types and the Sung 'Celadon' demanded by historical continuity, a link, moreover, that can be clearly perceived by the eye and the touch of the observer.

What we have already said about the wealth of glazes that Chinese scientific ignorance managed to produce, is especially true of the hyaline glazes of the SUNG DYNASTY (A.D. 960–1279), a period perhaps deserving particular attention for this reason alone. The potter has suddenly struck, as it were, a jade mine and produced glazes comprising the numberless shades of this precious gift of Nature. Rearranging by means of fire certain natural elements, he has now learned to make utensils which at the first glance and touch seem to be of jade and emit the same ringing sound.

But the nobility and variety of forms that the hand of the potter now knows how to produce must also be given serious consideration. The classical serenity that we find in Sung painting, the deliberate search for simple and universal expression, characterize all the artistic tendencies of the time and therefore also the products of all the kilns. This is a stylistic consciousness which we can use freely in assigning a date to these ceramics, since we have good reason to believe that some of the kilns went on working, without any change in the quality of their products, until well into the following YUAN DYNASTY (A.D. 1280–1368), and even till the time of the Mings, that is to say until the trend towards baroque began to influence all forms.

This SUNG-YUAN period might well be called the stoneware period, even if 'porcellaneous', because, if we can rely on the numerous references in Chinese sources and the deductions we can draw from them, the production of earthenware practically ceased, while porcelain (in the sense *we* give to the term) was not yet at this time one of the glories of the potter's art. Yet, if we examine each type separately, we shall see how near to porcelain we already are and how doubtful are the theories of European purists, in view of the delicacy of certain types.

Nevertheless we are at last beginning to find ourselves on firmer ground as regards dates and provenance.

With their deep interest in all ceramics and their taste for Chinese art, British scholars have devoted much study to this problem, often visiting the places mentioned in the classics. An interesting method of research has been applied to some very large heaps (one might almost call them small hills) in the vicinity of the kilns. These naturally consist of the refuse from the kilns, but among the shards defective pieces have also been found, still miraculously intact or fused with the saggars (boxes of refractory clay) in which they were placed in the kiln. By means of a meticulous system of excavation, not unlike that used for the various super-imposed layers at Troy, which made it possible to leave them intact, it has been possible in some cases to establish an exact scheme of development for each furnace. This has proved very useful in solving the problems presented by porcelain dating from later periods, problems due to the bad Chinese habit of marking them with completely arbitrary dates. Unfortunately, even this promising scientific beginning has had to be interrupted, so that systematic research has so far only skimmed the question of the great Sung kilns. In one or two rare cases an inscription underneath the glaze helped the scholars, as happened with the Ting-yao bowl belonging to the Percival David Foundation in London, on which not only the date, but the place of manufacture and the name of the artisan, are given.

The various types of ceramics produced during this period are so numerous as to disconcert even the most careful scholar, who finds himself groping in the dark as regards the development of each of these types. The general characteristic of the whole group is the hard and resounding 'body', often containing kaolin, but changing colour when subjected to the heat of the kiln. The decorations are similar to those of the T'ang period, executed, that is to say, by means of engraving, pressure or painting. The glaze is always of the local feldspathic type and the piece is baked only once in the 'great fire', and almost invariably reveals a small portion of bare body at the base. To produce determined effects, the colours are often modified on one and the same article, and in many types an attempt has been made to obtain crackle on the glaze by cooling the kiln quickly and then filling the thin network with colouring matter.

*

From the numerous references in the Chinese classics we can judge the importance of the potter's status at this time. We learn, in fact, that a certain number of kilns worked for the Imperial family. The ceramics produced by these centres, classified and anotated with an abundance of details by Chinese writers, are known as 'Classical Ceramics' and include the Yüeh, already described when we were dealing with the Five Dynasties, and the mysterious Ch'ai. As for the others, we will try to describe them one by one.

Ju-yao. This is the kind most lauded by Chinese art historians and it was produced at Juchow on the Ju River, in Western Honan. The body is of hard stoneware which turned to a dark ivory colour on contact with fire, and is covered by a beautiful, thick glaze with delicate nuances ranging from a gentle greenish blue to sky blue. This glaze is sometimes crackled and is as pleasing to the touch as live flesh, a property which it shares, even if only to a lesser degree, with all Sung glazes, and which was the special delight of the Chinese. Two pieces in the collection at the Imperial Palace bear the inscription: 'For the imperial caress of Chien Lung'.

On the bases of cups and other receptacles we often find the so-called 'spur-marks', these being the marks left by the tiny 'spurs' that supported the object during the firing. Much confusion has been caused by erroneous interpretations of these marks and of the special names given to the various forms of crackle (such as 'crab's leg', 'caviar', 'cracked ice'), as well as by attempts to describe the colours, so that we are not now in a position to affirm with certainty that the type of ceramics we have examined is really Ju-yao, so highly esteemed by the classics.

Ko-yao and *Kuan-yao* are very similar as regards body and glaze. Both are made of a hard stoneware turned to a blackish brown by the action of fire, and are covered with a thick glaze showing irregular crackle. *Kuan-yao* means 'official ceramics' and was presumably produced for the first time in the neighbourhood of K'aifeng and then, after the transfer of the seat of the Dynasty to the South, in 1127, at Hangchow. *Ko-yao*, on the other hand, was made at Lung-ch'uan in the province of Chekiang after 1227. The colours of the glaze range from a cool grey through various warmer tones to a brownish or greenish grey. The difference between the two types lies in the quality of the glaze and the crackle. The surface of *Kuan* is like slightly opaque jade, whereas *Ko* has a more glassy brilliance. In *Ko* pieces the crackle usually has finer dividing lines than in *Kuan*. We would warn over-enthusiastic collectors that excellent copies of both these types were made during the Yung Chen period (A.D. 1723–1735).

L'ung-ch'uan-yao, as the name shows, comes from the same locality as *Ko-yao*. The Chinese texts would lead us to suppose that the factory was founded by the younger brother of the creator of *Ko* (*Ko* means 'elder brother'), and if this was the case, we can only conclude that the enterprising young man must have been endowed with considerable talent. His products have come down to us under the name of 'Celadon' and have reached most parts of the civilized world. European museums display specimens with silver mountings in the Gothic style or with settings worthy of the most precious jewels, while the University of Oxford possesses a bowl bequeathed to New College by a bishop in 1530. The Mohammedan world must have shown great interest in this kind of ceramics, for the museum at Istanbul has many beautiful specimens from the former Sultans' collections and excavations near Cairo have brought numerous pieces to light.

The body of this type is hard and grey, turned to a beautiful reddish brown by firing, while the thickness varies considerably. Frequently the glaze, in various olive-green tones, leaves certain decorations in relief uncovered, thus revealing all the beauty of the marvellous ground. It is impossible to define the colour of the glaze otherwise than by the word 'Celadon', the origin of which is rather curious. This type of ceramics became fashionable in France at the beginning of the seventeenth century, in the early days of the craze for the bucolic *genre*. A young shepherd named Celadon appeared on the Parisian stage draped in a mantle of the same colour as *Lung-ch'uan-yao*, and as Chinese names are so difficult to pronounce . . . in the following century the Encyclopaedists described 'celadon' as a colour—'green mingled with white'.

There is another type called 'Northern Celadon', but no one knows why it is so called. It has a thin and almost transparent body covered with an oyster-green glaze. Exquisitely decorated, it is one of the finest types of the whole family (Plate 22).

The kilns at Lung-ch'uan continued working until the early years of the Ming Dynasty, producing pieces which in the main were heavier and of a more Baroque conception. The Japanese, who have a great liking for this kind of ceramics, still manufacture beautiful pieces, many of which are unfortunately difficult to distinguish from the Sung and Ming models.

Ting-yao. The best way of describing this type is to say that it is the successor of the beautiful white T'ang porcelain already mentioned and at the same time the predecessor of the great *Blanc de Chine* family of the Ming Dynasty. Nevertheless, in actual fact it differs from both and it is this difference that deprives it of the right to be called porcelain, even though the material remains white when exposed to the direct action of heat (that is to say, on the rims of bowls and other receptacles, which were placed in the kiln upside-down), and is very thin. But alas! it cannot claim to be transparent.

The unglazed rims are almost invariably concealed by bronze mounts, which those who examine them should always remove, as often they hide chipped edges. The under-glaze decorations are always very beautiful, consisting of *graffiti* freely drawn on the body before treatment, probably executed with little bamboo sticks.

The broad, sharp points of these achieve almost calligraphic effects of depth which, after glazing, give great richness to the designs, representing water-lilies and other flowers, ducks and fish. Patterns applied by pressure are also frequent. At certain points the layer of glaze tends to thicken, thus revealing its hyaline tone, sometimes ivory, sometimes a watery green. These thickened portions of glaze, looking like drops of water on the skin, are called 'tears'.

Before the seat of government was transferred to the South, the above-mentioned type was made at Ting-chow, in the province of Hopei; later, the centre of manufacture was near Chi-chow in the province of Kiangsi. Similar kinds were produced in Kiangsu and Anhui and all are classified under the general name of 'Ting-type ceramics' (Plate 21).

Chün-yao, on the other hand, comes from Northern Honan. Among the monochrome Sung ceramics it stands out owing to its red and cyclamen-coloured spots emerging from a thick layer of glaze ranging in colour from a delicate greyish blue to the darkest hues of a threatening sky. The type comprises diversities of quality as great as the diversity of colours, the finest pieces being made of light-grey material very similar to porcelain, while the coarser pieces are of rough 'biscuit' of a yellowish colour. In all of them the glaze seems to have been just poured over the body and left to solidify on contact. The spots of colour are due to oxidization. The finest specimens bear numbers, from one to ten, but the meaning of these is still obscure.

The so-called 'soft Chün' is normally attributed to the Yuan Dynasty without any plausible reason. The

attribution is based on the vague and somewhat doubtful hypothesis that, as the Ming Dynasty drew nearer,
grès tended to become softer, becoming once again like
earthenware. Nevertheless, 'soft Chün' displays a magnificent luminous glaze, sky blue in colour, and the
body is in reality hard, though the high percentage of
sand in the material gives an impression of softness.
(The Chinese call it *Sha-tai*, which means 'body of
sand'.)

A type of ceramics which perhaps deserves our
special attention is that which the modern Chinese have
chosen to call *Ying-ching* ('shadow blue') and which that
great scholar and patron of art, Sir Percival David,
prefers to call *Ching Pai*. The best specimens have fine
white bodies, so transparent as to deserve to be called
'porcelain'. Numerous bowls and vases bear incised or
pressed decorations very like those on *Ting-yao*, while
the glaze, of a greenish-blue transparence, throws the
designs into high relief. An interesting fact is that this
glaze is sometimes used, with striking effect, by artisans
whom we might well call the sculptors of porcelain,
for in this ware powerful small pieces of sculpture have
been found.

This type has been found all over China and in Korea,
and its exact place of origin remains doubtful. The re-
searches made by the late Archibald Brankston tended
to show that the greater part of the specimens originally
came from the province of Kiangsi, or, more precisely,
from a locality not far from what was soon to become
the great centre of porcelain manufacture under the
Ming Dynasty.

Recently the suggestion has been put forward that
this type may be the mysterious *Ch'ai yao* of the Five

Dynasties which we have already mentioned. But the fact that what we have until now called *Ying-ching* comprises, in addition to very fine pieces, coarsely executed and badly glazed specimens, certainly does not tally with the exalted descriptions of *Ch'ai yao* given by the classics.

The province of Kiangsi is also said to be the place of origin of a type attributed to the Yuan Dynasty and called *Shu-fu*. It may be conceded that it is really porcelain, as is the case with *Ying-ching*, with which it has close affinity, and the characters *Shu Fu*, meaning 'Privy Council', are often impressed underneath the glaze, as if forming part of the floral decoration. Nevertheless the finest specimens (Plate 23) are usually without this trade mark. The peculiar shade of the glazes is a harbinger of the blue and white series of the following dynasty, but the body is an echo of the elegant beauty of Sung and T'ang ceramics—which, incidentally, provided most of the inspiration for the following periods.

*

We now come to a group of Sung ceramics standing outside the 'classic' group and for that reason held by the Chinese to be of inferior rank and looked upon rather condescendingly. Foreign scholars, on the other hand, notice a pleasing spontaneity of form and decoration in these types and consequently derive from them a feeling of completeness more satisfactory than completeness itself. The beautiful decorations beneath the glaze of *Tz'u-chow* are often masterpieces of drawing and invention, inspired by a profound observation of Nature. Very few Sung pieces have such nobility of form and decoration as the vase, now in Washington, reproduced in Plate 20. And here, once again, we are faced with a problem. Many believe that the technique of freehand painting underneath the glaze that we see here for the first time was copied from the Persians and this, despite the difficulty of admitting that a nation of painters in an age of splendour like the Sung Dynasty should have had to look elsewhere to find the necessary inspiration for such an obvious development.

The name of the type reveals its place of origin: Tz'u-chow in the province of Hopei, where the porcelain and stoneware industries still flourish today. It has a hard, porcellaneous body in colours ranging from light grey to brown. The decorations are sometimes superimposed on the glaze, but more often they are executed on top of the 'slip', with vigorous strokes of the brush in a blackish-brown tone. The glaze is usually ivory white, though we sometimes find a transparent turquoise-blue glaze beneath which the black decorations produce a decidedly Persian effect. These turquoise-blue vases have often been attributed to the Ming period, but the style of the decorations and the forms themselves are closer to the Sung.

Temmoku is the name given by the Japanese and early Western scholars to a type of ceramics that the Chinese call *Chien-yao*. British scholars have studied it from close at hand on the sites of the kilns at Chien-yang in the province of Fukien. It is the favourite type with the Japanese. Here, too, the thick, blackish-brown glaze pours heavily down over the vessel, almost invariably stopping before it reaches the foot. Metallic gleams, like flashes of light, which the Chinese call 'hare's fur', often enliven the glaze. The body is very dark, almost black, and the pieces have a forbidding appearance rarely relieved by a ring of white glaze round the mouth or by longitudinal stripes.

Ceramics very similar to these were made in China under the Sungs in Kiangsu and Northern Honan, where the Chinese often call them 'Black Ting'. Of all this family, too, there exist excellent modern imitations, made not only in Japan, but also in China, in the very province of Fukien.

*

Among these less-exalted types we would mention that known as *Chü-lo-hsien*, discovered in a locality in the province of Hopei that for centuries (since 1108) had been under water. As the Yellow River had recently changed its course again, a French dealer from Peking followed the tracks of one of the men who provided him with wares, and found, buried in the mud of the old bed of the river, numerous pieces in stoneware with ivory glazes and grey bodies. The water had left rusty marks upon them, which, like the patina of time on bronzes, only added to their fascination. It is impossible to say whether these pieces were made on the spot, or else brought to the once-important city from kilns in the vicinity. In any case this group of objects at last gives us a really positive date: we know, without a shadow of doubt, that they must have been made before 1108. And what other type of Sung ceramics can give us as much as that?

*

Having reached this point, the author has to tackle an embarrassing problem and find a solution to the question involved in the title of this book. How far can we extend the conception of 'Chinese art'? To what extent can we fulfil the obligation we have undertaken? The Chinese maintain that the appreciation of all beauty is a matter of knowledge (and, therefore, of truth), going far beyond ordinary personal taste; but even this conception, like everything else in the realm of truth, has ill-defined limits, a frontier that remains invisible until we have crossed it. How much of the production of the MING and CHING DYNASTIES (A.D. 1386–1911) can still be described as 'art'? Quite arbitrarily, the author proposes to adopt a 'system of gradual diminution', coherent so far as regards *his* truth (since in human affairs even truth, like taste, can be personal), begging those whose truth is different to bear with him.

The Ming Dynasty was the great period of Chinese porcelain. A whole city was completely dedicated to the production of this material, now at last pure even according to the exacting standards of the West. The factories of Ching-te-chen (Kiangsi), soon to become the biggest centre of porcelain production in the world, turned out a marvellous white porcelain known by the name of the third Ming Emperor, Yung Lo (A.D. 1403–1424), which still shows reminiscences of Sung ceramics, such as, for example, the 'tears', not unlike those on Ting products (Plate 25).

The time is at hand when painting in cobalt beneath the glaze appears. Henceforth the art of the potter, that is to say of the man who shaped the piece, passes into the hands of the painter, who decorates it and gives it its wonderful colours. Some of the first specimens are a happy combination of both arts (Plate E). Even in this field, great confusion in the matter of dates caused considerable panic among the first collectors. With cheerful impudence the potters of the following dynasty marked their wares with the seals of the early and middle Ming periods, since from the days of the Emperor Hsüan Te (A.D. 1426–1435) blue and white porcelain begins to be dated by means of a special mark. The vigour of the painting thus remains the only sure guide: in the early Ming period, flowers, fish, human figures and animals are executed by real artists, with a strength, sureness and virtuosity that unhappily decline even before the richness of the beautiful cobalt. This colour was obtained with the help of minerals imported from the Mohammedan world—to which these types of porcelain returned in large quantities, taking the place of 'Celadon' in the export market. There are collections at Istanbul and Teheran containing material the study of which enables us to restore order in the chaos created by the light-hearted potters of the Ching Dynasty. It is sad to have to record that commercial requirements influenced the forms in a definitely negative sense. The decline of this white and blue porcelain begins in the reign of Wan Li (A.D. 1573–1619), when exports achieved really disconcerting proportions. The colour that reached its apex under Cheng Te (1506–1521) and Chia Ching (1522–1566) began to degenerate. By now the Dutch had entered the trade and the prototypes for their own production of blue and white porcelain made their first appearance in the houses of the burghers.

Akin to this type was a porcelain with red and brown,

instead of blue, decorations beneath the glaze, obtained by using copper. This type perhaps came from the kilns at Chün, since, as we have already seen, the secret of producing red and violet spots on a blue body was known there. The technique of combining red with blue developed slowly and somewhat later, because the two colours require different degrees of temperature.

*

During the Ming period, in addition to white porcelain, numerous monochrome types in other colours are found: red, brown, black, dark blue, turquoise blue, green and yellow. The leading role in Ming production was played by porcelain with 'enamel painting', i.e. with decorations applied on top of the glaze. There are many specimens of outstanding beauty in which the meticulous technique has not yet robbed the painting of its vigour and the requirements of purchasers have not yet begun to influence the elegance of Chinese form. The rich gamut of colours used, obtained by empirical local means, is yet another revelation of the inventiveness peculiar to Chinese potters; to the colours mentioned above are added an aubergine violet and a liver red. The Chinese call this enamelled porcelain *Wu-tsai*, i.e. 'Five Colours'—a term which, while defining its polychrome nature, is inadequate as regards the numbers of colours used. It required a complicated firing technique, since colours applied on top of the glaze can stand only lower and varying temperatures.

A variant of this type of porcelain is enamelled directly on the 'biscuit'. The bowl in Sir Percival David's collection is a magnificent specimen of this and

PLATE 28. Cock in porcelain, white on brown. K'ang Hsi period. Height 3 1/8 inches (8 cm.). *Collection of Dott. Alessandro Campilli, Rome.*

PLATE 29. Porcelain vase. *Famille noire.* Height 18⅞ inches (48 cm.).
Collection of His Excellency Giovanni Gronchi, Rome.

PLATE 30. Figure in stone. Shang-Yin Dynasty. Height 5½ inches (15 cm.).
Collection of Mr. T. Y. King, Hongkong.

PLATE 31. Stone relief of a phoenix. Han Dynasty.
In situ at Chü Hsien in Szechwan.

can perhaps be considered the last authentic work of art by a Chinese potter (Plate 27).

The technique of applying enamel colours to porcelain bodies is akin to that used for stoneware and earthenware during this dynasty, and the Chinese call it *Fa Hua*. Divisions forming designs were made on the 'biscuit' and these were then filled with enamel. Sometimes the enamels were applied without the use of such *'cloisons'*, especially in the case of figures, in which the face and hands stand out, these being left unenamelled. Such figures were often used for embellishing temples, and earthenware roof-tiles were also enamelled.

To the late Ming period we must also assign the first appearance of the *Blanc de Chine* series (seventeenth century), the most important of the ceramics made outside Ching-te-cheng and coming from Te Hua in Fukien. Here, too, we are faced with a problem, since no traces have been left that could explain the development of such technical perfection. The body and the enamel are fused in a perfect harmony and not without reason many believe that *Te Hua* or Fukien is the most beautiful of all porcelains (Plate 24).

It is difficult to date it with certainty, even if we follow up every possible trace. A little Fukien figure dressed in the uniform of a Dutch soldier of 1650, now in the British Museum, has been the focal point around which scholars have been more or less groping for years. It would perhaps be better to rely on a certain criterion of the form, a criterion which long and loving practice makes it possible to achieve and which, in the end, is often the best guide. This is yet another aspect of that faculty of judgment which enables us to 'feel' the strength of painting, to 'guess' the material, its weight, colour and substance. It is a knowledge relegated to an obscure corner of our being, independent of all reasoning and absolutely direct. The Chinese express the directness of its action by the phrase *K'ai men djien shan*, meaning 'Open the door and see the mountain'. They give more importance than we do to this faculty, because they believe more than we do that certain perceptions must be accepted at least to the same degree with which we accept others known to emanate from the brain.

*

As regards the conception of 'art' in ceramics during the last of the dynasties, the Ch'ing or Manchu, the early part of this period, the reign of the Emperor K'ang Hsi (1662–1722) deserves to be remembered for its return to the nobility of form, for the exquisite use of monochrome glazes that had started during the Ming period and gave greater emphasis to the forms, and for certain fine modellings of birds, animals and human figures (Plate 28). Production of most of the Ming types continued during this period and in particular that of blue and white porcelain, which, however, lost much of the beauty of its colouring and acquired an excessively delicate glaze. The K'ang Hsi period is also the period of the French 'families':

Famille noire: Enamelling in three colours on a black ground previously applied directly on the 'biscuit'. These pieces, which, it is true, are very rare, still fetch exaggerated prices today, though the painting is very vivacious and the technique very complicated (Plate 29).

Famille verte: Porcelain mostly with a white glazed ground, on which green enamels predominate over aubergine, violet, yellow, blue and red.

Famille jaune: Like the *famille noire*, this is a continuation of Ming porcelain, enamelled directly on the 'biscuit', but the predominating colour for the ground is in this case a greenish yellow.

With these techniques and these colours not only receptacles were produced, but also delightful little figures, invariably with the faces and hands unenamelled.

On the other hand, the potters of the Emperor Yung Cheng (1722–1735) must have succumbed to the fascination of the beautiful Sung pieces that came into their hands, for the most important of their products are mere imitations of these ceramics, especially of the *Ko* and *Kuan* types. But it was also during the reign of this Emperor that pink was finally discovered, by adding gold in the form of a precipitate. As soon as it appeared on porcelain, the French made a 'family' of it: the *famille rose*. Finely enamelled plates (certainly for use in the palace) were made, decorated with human figures, birds and flowers, with pink as the predominating colour, while the backs of the plates were a fine dark red. This type, known as 'ruby back', together with the *famille noire*, had the greatest success as regards price. Now French influence was felt everywhere. Enamels on a copper ground were executed in Canton in brazen imitation of a completely foreign technique. Even some of the designs are foreign. The production of the 'Compagnie des Indes' porcelain began. Europeans are amazed by the beauty of Chinese material and go into ecstasies over the exotic delicacy of the decorations, completely unaware of the past glories of Chinese art.

With Ch'ien Lung (1736–1795), the Empire achieved its maximum and final political importance, to such an extent that it aroused the envy even of powerful visitors. But the new atmosphere these visitors brought with them scattered the last remains of Chinese artistic greatness even though the Emperor himself undertook a pilgrimage into the great past of his country, engraving nostalgic poems on ancient porcelain. It was the period of snuff-boxes, of glass looking like the finest porcelain, of enamelled basins decorated with painted figures of Dutch soldiers looking like Chinese. Strange porcelain cylinders, fitting one into the other, appeared; by turning one of them, one got the impression that the little figures incised on the other were marching over a bridge. Perhaps the last blow to the art of the Chinese potter was dealt when he tried to solve the purely Western problem of kinetics.

CHAPTER FIVE

Sculpture

WHEN we turn to works of sculpture, we find another proof of the inadequacy of the archaeological excavations hitherto made. It is true that as a result of systematic excavations on the Shang-Yin sites between 1928 and the Sino-Japanese war much information was obtained on sculpture of that period, but we are completely in the dark as to the following years down to the Han Dynasty and it would almost seem that the expressive urge of a people so traditionalist as the Chinese came to a sudden stop. On the other hand, the importance of the sculpture on stone at Anyang, attributed to the SHANG-YIN DYNASTY (?1766–1122? B.C.), the bold conception of certain of the larger specimens and the exquisite ornamental borders are really perplexing. One is tempted to think that it is wrong to consider the Shang-Yin period as that in which not only sculpture, but the whole of Chinese art, began. And when we consider these works together with those in jade, pottery and bronze, we cannot help feeling that with the Shang-Yin period a great era in Eastern Asian art reached its apex, immediately before the years of silence that followed. While the very works of the Shang-Yin period confirm our suspicion that our ignorance of earlier times is due to an archaeological gap, we are still groping in the dark as regards the Chou period, which lasted a thousand years, towards the latter half of which it is presumed that the first symptoms of an artistic renaissance began to appear. In the classical texts we find only vague references to sculpture on stone in this period; they speak of large figures of animals and servants which it is supposed lined the avenues leading to the tombs. But as no such works have ever been found, the doubt arises whether zealous copyists may not have attributed to the Chou period what, as we shall see later, really belongs to the Han.

The marble and stone Shang-Yin sculptures offer a vast and interesting field for study. Although the conception is bold, the officially recognized pieces lack the accurate finish found in the bronzes and it is clear that this material was not held in great esteem. They are rarely more than two feet high, for the most part representing animals—tortoises, bears or dragons—and very rarely the human figure. They are all adorned with carved symbols not unlike those found on bronze utensils and shards of pottery coming from the same tombs. Despite the careless finish, these specimens have the same robustness we have noticed in the bronzes and their decorations express deep reverence (Plate 30).

Fragments of what must have been the finest Shang-Yin sculpture were discovered at Peking in the shops of dealers, who had every interest in being evasive as to their place of origin and therefore afforded no help. (One can but speculate as to the Elysian Fields to which a receiver of works stolen by tomb robbers might have been able to guide us in the good old times and regret the laziness that induced us to buy them instead from the dealers.) Thus, while it is true that this double source of material of two types differing somewhat from each other (the 'unofficial' fragments are much more delicately finished) offers an interesting field, it is even truer that it deprives us of all hope of achieving concrete knowledge of a period which we have come to accept as having been archaeologically investigated. Moreover, this twofold source divides the scholars into two groups: those who attribute considerable importance to Chinese sculpture, and those whose embarrassment as regards Chinese sculpture in general begins with the Shang period. This is a subject which deserves a more detailed analysis.

The puzzled scholars are at pains to explain that sculpture was never considered by the Chinese to be a real art, since they were accustomed to expressing their thoughts by means of the brush and were therefore incapable of expending the longer time and greater physical effort required when working with the chisel. We will leave it to the reader to judge the plausibility of this argument, and also the works of these so-called artisans. Personally we think that the error is due to the fact that many people are unable to see their own conditioned ideas as regards sculpture from another point of view, the emotions which the Chinese sculptors successfully tried to express being too remote from their own sensibility. Like all other sculpture, Chinese sculpture, when it achieves grandeur, is inspired by a religious fervour, but in this case by a religious fervour which, being of a different nature, acts in a different manner. There could be no better illustration of this difference of religious conception than that offered by a comparison between Plates 36 and 37, and this despite the fact that both contain certain plastic elements differentiating them from traditional Western sculpture inspired by Hellenistic ideals. Whereas the Indian deity proudly displays its eroticism (the prime factor in its creation) without for all that repudiating the element in which it is created, stone, the Chinese deity expresses within the same limits a greater dignity and a gentle sweetness. In neither case do we find any trace of the Greek attempt to convert stone into flesh, although the artist has tried to express the human and divine attributes as completely as possible. We shall see how in China the progressive attempts to debase wood and stone so as to make them resemble as far as possible human flesh is a symptom of the decline and fall of Chinese sculpture—a decline and fall which will appear illogical to those who in their own country have seen exactly the opposite happen.

But those who persist in assigning to Chinese sculpture little more than an ancillary role have better powder and shot than this for their well-placed batteries. Combing the Chinese texts, they remind us of the contempt in which the scholar-writers held all Chinese artists who dared to express their sentiments by any other medium than the brush, the only instrument worthy of real artists. Inevitably 'art for art's sake' must have been among the favourite mottoes of the Chinese scholar. His contempt for sculpture thus became greater when he discovered that statues served a definite purpose, namely religion, just as he was ready to despise the painters who debased their brushes by making them fulfil a function such as the glorification of a god.

*

Nevertheless, there are moments in the evolution of Chinese sculpture when such indifference might have been justifiable. Of the years following the Buddhist epoch we shall have time to speak later; here we will limit ourselves to an examination of what is known to us of the sculpture of the HAN DYNASTY (206 B.C.–A.D. 220), in order to see whether our premise is applicable to it.

In the province of Shansi we find an avenue flanked by large stone animals leading to a typical terraced tomb containing the remains of a cavalry general, one Huo K'iu Ping, who died in 117 B.C. This is the largest and oldest group hitherto found. The most important item is a horse trampling a man to death and its monumental conception is so unexpected that it is disconcerting. The remaining animals, on the other hand, seem clumsy and static, with that fixed dignity which, by invoking the idea of eternity, illuminates the more delicately finished Egyptian sculptures. Here we have to do with winged monsters who preserve their animal attributes, and in this kind of sculpture there is no trace of evolution or change during the four hundred years of the Dynasty. The beautiful winged chimaeras, elegant even if somewhat mastodontic, and recalling all the power of the bronze animals of the late Chou period, are nevertheless attributed to the fifth century. Their inner dynamism and the thirst for movement which emanates from them make it almost impossible to believe that they were evolved from the Han animals.

We have a lot more to say about another field of Han sculpture, the bas-reliefs adorning the princely tombs of that period. The technique used would suggest leaving all consideration of them to the chapter dealing with painting, but the material in which they are carved makes it necessary to deal with them here. The carving, on stone and clay, is an imitation of brushwork and this, together with the nature of the scenes reproduced, has led many scholars to believe that these bas-reliefs were accurate copies of mural frescoes existing in the palaces of the deceased, reproduced for their delectation in a material capable of defying eternity. We thus find ourselves once again confronted with a by no means negligible manifestation of art having as its sole purpose the delectation of the dead, since the very rigorous funerary regulations forbade anyone to enter the tomb once the deceased had been immured in it.

Noteworthy in these bas-reliefs are the verve, the movement, the power of the draughtsmanship: human figures and animals, hunters and hunted creatures. Confucian sages, dragons and other fantastic Taoist animals, drastically stylized, seem as if they had been carved with a steel needle. There is nothing primitive, no sign of adaptation to the material: this is the continuation of a profound graphical experience suddenly made manifest by a new means. The use of the new medium of expression seems to have been widespread, since tombs of this kind have been discovered in Shantung, Szechwan, Honan and Hopei (Plate 31).

If, in view of its peculiar graphical nature, we leave the carvings on stone we have just discussed and return to Han sculpture in the round, the best we can say of it (apart from its monumental purpose) is that it established the rules for that attempt at expression within the material which we have already mentioned. Devoid of any marked religious content, statuary has nothing further to say. But perhaps it was precisely because he had no other preoccupations that the sculptor could allow the material in which he was working to express itself on its own account and to inspire him with great respect. For us Han sculpture is important for yet another reason, if the condemnation of the black Hui-hsien pottery from the late Chou period should ever prove to be valid: for the first time the representation of the human figure becomes fairly frequent. The tombs are filled with figures in baked and glazed clay of the human beings sacrificed by the Shangs and that shows us the extent of the decay of a very ancient, if sanguinary, belief. The disincarnate Supreme Being has become too nebulous; for a long time past representations of him and of Shê on bronzes have become purely decorative. The times are ripe for a new belief.

Buddha, already transformed by Indian idolaters, now makes his first appearance in human form. In ideal representations he wears a Greek tunic and has the curly hair of an Apollo, as a result of the influence exercised by the sculptures left by Alexander the Great in Northern India or, more convincingly, by Alexandrine Roman sculptors. This new god, repellent at first sight to a people who had hitherto believed in an incorporeal divinity, gradually became familiar and more comprehensible precisely on account of his form. The fall of the Hans, the momentary disorganization of the State-supported Confucians, the sufferings of the people in a disastrous political situation, resulted in the rapid and grateful acceptance of a god who promised eternal bliss after death. The gates of the Empire were thrown open and allowed free ingress to the Indian propagandists who brought with them, as their valid supports, statues of their gods as well as sculptors: artists who were at the same time teachers. Proselytes and artisans flocked round them and soon Buddha assumed definitely Chinese features, as also happened with

Avalokiteshvara, as masculine as any Buddhist divinity could be, who was later transformed into Kwan Yin, the goddess of mercy. These features had an austerity of form and a universal spirituality such as only the Chinese could give in so high a degree to the representation of the new concept: that of the man-god. We have reason to believe that this first success of Indian missionaries, this almost immediate assimilation, gave the Indian Buddhists the illusive impression that they had won a great victory, which, very naturally, they interpreted in the light of their own development. But it was not long before they realized that their practical neighbours had done no more than add yet another religion to the lukewarm beliefs they already held. Whatever the subsequent developments, however, once the first shock had been overcome, the representation of divinity in human form soon found favour. And this was certainly the basis of what may well be called a religious as well as an aesthetic revolution. The Chinese became accustomed to it with that incredible faculty of adaptation which is the outstanding individual characteristic of the race and the true yardstick of its intelligent conception of life.

*

The advent of this new manner (new, at all events, for us, since we have to take the objects found as our basis) occurred in China under the rule of the Wei Tartars, who governed Northern China during the period we call the SIX DYNASTIES (A.D. 220–589), or more precisely between 386 and 557. About the middle of the fifth century, violent persecution resulted in the destruction of all works executed by the Buddhists before that time, and it is for this reason that our first discoveries of the finest Buddhist sculpture consisted of works that are already completely Chinese, dating, that is to say, from the fifth century onwards (Plates 32, 33).

The biggest repositories of these great sculptures were the caves in the slopes of Mount Yüng-Kang in the province of Shansi and in the neighbourhood of the Wei capital, Heng An. In this score of sandstone caves the first Buddhists carved what are perhaps the most monumental statues the world has ever seen, since some of the Buddhas are almost seventy feet high. Bodhisattvas (among them Avalokiteshvara and Maitreya) were carved out of the live rock, as were the eighteen Lohans, the winged angels and all the minor deities, freely borrowed from the Hindu religion and forming the rich iconography of Mahayana Buddhism. But the Chinese quickly evolved felicitous adaptations in their own manner, giving these creatures a peculiarly Chinese stamp. And on this point it will be well to dwell a little longer.

What strikes us most in these Yüng-Kang statues is the affirmation of a style that binds them all together like a steel wire. Chinese formalism, which in its time had given the bronzes their gerarchical values, now organizes their latent creative impulses in a circumscribed manner of expression. The theme is as fixed as the pivot of Confucius, for which reason the variations, the minor deviations and the spasmodic suggestions are of the greatest importance, because they belong to the kingdom of man. The gods are static, cold, enormous, solid as the mountain against which they stand. Their attitudes are impersonal as the Milky Way and their robes fall in folds that cannot be anything but austere, austere to the point of boredom. These are the themes, the motives, belonging to eternity. The secret consists in creating suggestive variations and human evasions, while leaving the set theme intact; it consists in imparting to the impersonal attitude something that transcends not only the stone out of which the god is hewn, but the very nature of the sculptor, so that the countenance gives forth a smile divine rather than human. The secret consists in endowing the solidity of the forms and the massive immobility with a superhuman lightness that is almost movement; in giving, lastly, to the draperies an angularity so daring that it endows these gods and saints with a celestial dignity, closely bound, for reasons beyond our powers of perception, to geometry—just as the universe is bound up with geometry. At Yüng-Kang the Chinese sculptors were completely successful in achieving all this, just as they were successful in the caves of Lung Men, when the Tartars moved their capital elsewhere. There, the much harder stone allowed a greater refinement of detail and a return to the plastic form dear to the Hans—the bas-relief.

Another great centre of Wei sculpture was Tien Lung Shan, likewise in Shansi. The specimens found there are interesting also from a chronological point of view, since in these caves we can detect the first beginnings of that degeneration of stone into flesh of which we have already spoken in this chapter. We must consider this to have been the result of a vigorous offensive on the part of the Indian missionaries, leading to a certain weakening of the typical Chinese ideas. We shall see how, through this form of plastic expression, the Indians continued their aesthetic-religious offensive until the T'ang period, and this despite the fact that a close examination of the local annals by Western scholars shows that the Chinese fought strenuously against the new theories, whether spiritual or aesthetic. In the caves at Tien Lung Shan we find the divine bodies taking on the softness and roundness of flesh, while the draperies become mere textiles. The figures are no longer placed against the rock, but stand erect and isolated, as if trying to breathe with greater ease. Nevertheless, the general impression is still one of austerity, even though it may be more temperate. To this evolution has been given the name of that which, in the Six Dynasties, followed the Wei, the *Northern Ch'i* (A.D. 550–577), during the last years of which a further persecution of Buddhism caused serious destruction and brought about a temporary interruption of the spread of this faith.

*

The SUI DYNASTY (A.D. 589–618), which ushered in the great reunification of the Empire, witnessed a great renaissance in religious sculpture. The Emperor himself was a devout Buddhist, who ordered that the temples should be rebuilt and great works of sculpture executed. The Chinese annals, which had an exaggerated liking for statistics (and Mark Twain's opinion on this topic here finds its best confirmation), inform us that the number of sculptures ordered by this monarch amounted to 100,000.

If we wish to study this period, we must once again

return to the caves of Yunnan, Shantung and Szech-wan, where we find the specimens offering the greatest scope, since they were provided with inscriptions and dates; moreover, the other great works in stone, bronze, wood and lacquer that adorned the palaces have not survived the continual violence of persecutors. Though short, the period is important because of the strong official support resulting in the fulfilment of the in-structions given by the Indian missionaries four hun-dred years before to Chinese Buddhists. It closes the cycle of a style which may be called Wei because, although important deviations began to creep in in the fourth and fifth centuries, we still find specimens executed in the Wei style down to the end of the Sui period.

Nevertheless, the Sui renaissance brought noteworthy parallel innovations. The most important (the style of which takes its name from the Sui Dynasty) was the appearance of almost tubular bodies tending to restrict the play of the draperies which had had such a vital role in the Wei style. The new roundness sought for appropriate variations and the bodies were adorned with jewels. Since the purity of Buddha himself could not be disturbed, most of these ornaments were assigned to Avalokiteshvara, whose shape (probably in order to give greater prominence to the precious chains and belts studded with gems) became gradually more slender, thus initiating his pilgrimage towards femi-ninity (Plate 37).

To a certain extent the style had already established itself. Different localities show different trends. At Tien Lung Shan, as in the caves already mentioned, work continued. A Sui innovation appeared in the forms of

PLATE 32. Group in gilded bronze. Wei Dynasty (dated 518 A. D.).
Height 8⁷/₈ inches (22.5 cm.). *Musée Guimet, Paris.*

PLATE 33. Stone head of Buddha. Wei Dynasty.
W. R. Nelson Gallery of Art, Kansas City.

PLATE 34. Stone stele. T'ang Dynasty. Height 29½ inches (75 cm.).
Collection of M. Alphonse Kann, Paris.

PLATE 35. Marble torso. Sui Dynasty.
Height 5 $^7/_8$ inches (15 cm.). *Victoria &
Albert Museum, London.*

PLATE 36. *Yakshi* in sandstone. India,
100-25 B. C. *Museum of Fine Arts,
Boston (Mass.).*

the guardians protecting the gods, the most beautiful of which, however, were found near Anyang and bear the date 589. Caves were now plentiful in Shantung, but not all the surviving items were found in them. We also find votive offerings, often elaborately carved in high and low relief and nearly always with inscriptions consisting of Buddhist texts. They are large stone slabs, known as steles, part of which was generally hollowed out so as to form a kind of niche in which the divinity was placed. Brilliantly painted and repainted by donors as *ex-votos*, some of these were placed in temples beside the beautiful sculptures in wood and lacquer of which, unfortunately, only a few specimens remain. Very seldom does a wooden figure from this period come on the market and often, like all the wooden images from following periods, it bears traces of numerous superimposed layers of colour: green, red, blue and gold. But even in this respect the astute forger shows himself to be a master. To the corroded wood of old telephone poles he patiently applies layers of painting in various colours which the dealer brings to light with the aid of a little ivory knife in the presence of the potential purchaser, to inveigle him into concluding the affair.

*

In the chapter on the history of China we saw how the first rulers of the T'ANG DYNASTY (A.D. 618–906) put an end to the exaggerated patronage of Buddhist art by the Sui Emperor. That great warrior, the T'ang Emperor Tai Tsung, devoted all his artistic interests to the honourable companions of his activities, horses, ordering monumental effigies of six chargers which had carried him in battle and laying down that after his death they should be placed as supports to his funerary chamber. This predilection of so noble an Emperor for so noble an animal created a vogue for horses throughout the realm. Numerous thoroughbreds were imported from Bactria and the game of polo was introduced, in which both men and women took part, unless they preferred to watch the play of skilled foreign players wearing turbans (Plate 17). For the delectation of the dead, earthenware effigies of these players were placed in the tombs, together with tiny figures of maidservants, slaves, guards and animals.

The early years of the T'ang Dynasty witnessed the appearance of many non-Buddhist sculptures and a whole crop of Taoist works—that religion which abandoned its own precepts to follow the example of Buddhist propaganda, as well as a form of hieratical Buddhist organization. But with the advent of the Empress Wu there was another Indian invasion and an influx of non-Chinese blood entered into the national aesthetic ideas: a continual transfusion which occurred regularly at the end of every persecution. The exquisite statuette in wood of Maitreya in Plate 38 is almost completely Indian, though executed in China about a hundred and fifty years after the Indian creed had made its first appearance there.

This reversion to a greater affinity with our own sculpture has led most Western observers to consider the T'ang period as one of maturity in the field of sculpture. There were, of course, indigenous trends of a purely religious nature that contributed to this evolution, though it is difficult to establish how much, even of these, was imported. Moreover, there were various trends of this kind, differing considerably from one locality to another. Be that as it may, their contribution to the already mentioned works in the Tien Lung Shan caves is symptomatic of the general tendency. We find there a definite breaking away from the Wei past. The statues stand erect, the flesh covers the bones and the transparence of the draperies gives a delicate modelling to the bodies. No one physical detail dominates the others: the statue is a single harmonious whole. The figures and their attitudes are given a definite expression, such as to render their purpose and intentions immediately clear: the saints pray and worship the god dutifully; the guardians are ready to rush to the defence of their protégés; the semi-divine Bodhisattvas seem on the point of taking flight to higher spheres. The majesty of these supernatural creatures has vanished and been replaced by a more mundane elegance. Soon afterwards, perhaps because the priests in authority became aware of it, a return to greater solemnity was ordered. The statues grew in dimensions, not only in breadth in order to conform with the T'ang ideal, but also in height. But never again will stone transcend the earthly nature of the sculptor. Henceforth every figure will remain human (Plate 39).

*

Inscriptions with relative dates are not found on sculptures after the middle of the eighth century, so that the chronology of the later T'ang works and those of the following period once more becomes that matter of intuition which is peculiar to Chinese art (and which, moreover, endows it with the perverse interest of uncertainty). This precarious state of affairs was made even worse by the return of sculpture, after the advent of the SUNG DYNASTY (A.D. 960–1279) to the styles of the past, a fashion which lasted, though with changes in the prototypes, throughout the Ming Dynasty. We must not forget that the Sung period did not encourage forms of expression that served a definite purpose, that the contempt of the scholars for functional art had spread to a large part of society and that Ch'an Buddhism, which had now ousted the traditional form, was averse to iconolatry. Caves containing Sung sculptures are few indeed and it was not until the northern part of China was conquered by the Tartars, still faithful to the traditional form of Buddhism, that religious sculpture came into its own again. Thus, instead of producing great statues like those in the caves of the North, the sculptors of this period returned to the beautiful old Wei and Ch'i forms. For the Chinese this was the first instance of a return to older artistic forms and, unfortunately, it became a popular precedent in all the fields of art. In this particular case the return was ruthlessly complete, so much so in fact that the exclusion of the votive stele reproduced in Plate 40 from the Wei group can be considered as recent, due to the circumspect study of this field made by expert scholars such as Oswald Sirén and Alfred Salmony.

Judging from the specimens found, one might conclude that at this time wood was considered the most suitable material for plastic expression, but unfortunately owing to the perishable nature of this material the oldest sculptures have all been lost. Nevertheless, the Southern Sungs allowed a wooden effigy of

PLATE C. Bowl in porcellaneous stoneware. *Chün Yao*. Sung Dynasty. Diameter 7 inches (18 cm.). *Collection of Marchese G. Litta-Modignani, Capalbio.*

Maitreya (which some consider to be a real Buddha, and not a Bodhisattva) to be placed among the decorations in their Ch'an temples. Such effigies belong to the T'ang tradition, though the features, in particular, have a more refined expression, in conformity with the general Sung tendency as revealed especially in painting, to which the sculptors turned for models and inspiration (Plate 41).

During the YUAN DYNASTY (A.D. 1280–1368) sculpture continued to follow the newer tradition and manner, to such an extent as to render useless any attempt to distinguish it. The typical lamaist sculptures in bronze, afterwards copied by the Lamaist Ching conquerors *ad nauseam*, made their first appearance at this time.

*

During the MING DYNASTY (A.D. 1368–1644) a second reversion to older forms took place, not only in sculpture, but also, as we shall see later, in painting. The Chinese conquerors of the Mongol despots were incapable of appreciating the refined and thoughtful style of the Sungs who, after all, had brought the country to disaster. They therefore returned to the T'angs, and so completely that it is difficult to distinguish a fine wooden Ming figure from its T'ang prototype.

In stone, too, there was a change that to a certain extent can be described as a reversion. Mastodontic stone animals line the approaches to the great Ming tombs in the environs of Peking. The Ming rulers embraced Confucianism with enthusiasm. This return to a pre-Buddhist form was a step in the right direction, but the necessary feeling was lacking: these animals no longer have the power and dynamism of those of the fifth century. They are large and massive, and nothing else.

Sculpture also invaded the workshops of the potters and in the course of time was engulfed in them. But during the Ming period it was still flourishing. To adorn the Buddhist temples large statues of the eighteen Lohans were carved, and since each of them had perforce to be different from the others, they provided excellent practice for the portraitists. Smaller statues, also in glazed ceramics, adorned the roofs, cornices and balustrades. Some are witty caricatures of the first Portuguese traders, whom the Chinese found very comical, on account both of their manners and their unduly florid appearance (Plate 42).

Chance (or perhaps something more than mere chance) willed that Western foreigners should preside over the final decay of this art, carrying it to the decorative extreme which accorded so well with the rococo tastes of our forefathers. When the Western layman hears Chinese sculpture mentioned, his thoughts at once turn to these horrible Lohans, or to the Eight Immortals cut out of pine roots, or to the carved head of a Chinese bed brought home by his grandfather after the Boxer rebellion. But he knows nothing of the greatness of Wei and T'ang sculpture, and nor did the Chinese themselves until recently, for it is only now that they are rediscovering these masterpieces, led through the caves in organized parties by those same fanatics who are organizing small provincial museums for the nationalistic education of the young, who until yesterday admired nothing but the technical inventions im-

ported into China from the West. Probably it is believed that a knowledge of the native genius for artistic
invention might stimulate the genius for modern forms
of scientific invention, which is the great need in
modern China, far greater than the need for a national
conscience.

CHAPTER SIX

Painting

PAINTING, more than any other branch of Chinese art, requires from the neophyte a complete abandonment of all his Western preconceptions. When he looks at a wall painting (*Chüan*, or, in Japanese, *Kakemono*), or cautiously unrolls a horizontal scroll (*Shou Chüan* or *Makimono*), he must never forget that the painter merely presents a 'poetical' arrangement of Nature, using the same instrument that he used for that other form of poetry—calligraphy.

The Chinese scholar, accustomed to relying on the brush for writing—in other words, for giving a definitive and simplified form to what were originally mere sketches of objects—uses it in the same way in order to set down the vision of what surrounds him. If we consider the matter from the point of view of evolution, we can imagine that the first clumsy attempts to translate the technique of writing into that of painting had as their first result a greater degree of accuracy and subsequently drew encouragement from the fact that this was the most suitable means of freeing the poet-painter from the fetters of inventive technique, and permitting him to express directly in a new and visible form what was the desire of his heart, that is to say, poetry. Naturally, that excludes those other attributes of painting which he lacked: the faithfulness of perspective, perfect modelling with the aid of the ingenious play of light and shade, those feats of virtuosity on which our painters rely in order to give material form to their work. When he looks at a Chinese painting, the neophyte must forget that, whereas the Western painter, before the advent of photography, used painting in order to reproduce and illustrate Nature as faithfully as possible, the Chinese painter always considered painting as a means of expressing an emotion—wonder, fear, the undefinable—that momentary inner vibration answering to the name of poetry. Which came first? The Chinese brush or the lyrical sentiment? Any attempt to reply to this question would involve us in useless discussions, but even if we refrain from drawing any conclusions from the examination of the paintings, the very way in which the Chinese artist set about his work shows that he used what he saw in Nature for purposes very different from those of mere reproduction.

Let us now try to follow mentally a scholar-painter as he gets ready to work and let us rid ourselves once and for all of the idea that we shall see him choosing a suitable place affording a view of the countryside and making measurements and creating a visual image of that part of the landscape which he intends to reproduce on his easel. If we do happen to find him in the open air, we shall see him wandering about the countryside, indulging in leisurely dreams, or, at the very most, making an occasional sketch to supplement his already exceptional powers of observation.

But it is in his simple, bare room that we shall see him at what for him is the most important moment. This is his refuge, far from all thoughts of the world. His first aim is to achieve peace of mind, because only in this way (as a famous twelfth-century painter once said) is it possible for him to feel in harmony with

Nature and to achieve perfect co-ordination of mind and hand. Forgetting his physical self, he seeks to absorb the rhythm of the continual renewal of Nature, to identify himself with eternity, to achieve that state of mind which is ideal for contemplation and reproduction, which will give serenity to his work—that serenity which comes from an absolute belief in the perfect ordering of things. It is this unshakable faith in the beauty of this order which allows him to make a free choice of his subject, from the ugly to the sublime. In Chinese painting we find an abundance of old men, horrible for us in their accentuated senility, of monsters and frightening creatures. The old men are there to remind us of the transitoriness of all human things, the others form counterparts to beauty, since in Nature everything is in equilibrium, and sometimes in an equilibrium of opposites reciprocally dependent on one another.

On a fine oblong table in front of our painter lie sheets of silk and of paper (since he will choose either one or the other according to the whim of the moment). Both of these materials are slightly absorbent, so that the signs he places upon them, like the cuts made by a chisel on stone, cannot be obliterated. Beside him, in a bowl resembling a severed bamboo trunk, are his brushes, with wooden handles and of various sizes: some of them very fine, others large and blunt with a sharp point above the swelling in the body. All these brushes, made of the hairs of hares, foxes or sables, are extremely delicate instruments, the point being so thin that it does not exceed the breadth of a single hair. Beside the artist, on the same side as the bowl, is the stone slab on which the solid ink is diluted with water until it acquires the necessary density—from raven black to a delicate dove grey. Hanging from the wall is a shelf for his seals and the implements for engraving them, since every painter is also an engraver of seals. Often he devises a new seal for a just-finished painting which gives him particular satisfaction. The seal comprises his name and sometimes a pseudonym. It is dipped into a little receptacle containing cinnabar and impressed at the end of calligraphical quotations or original poems, the purpose of which is to heighten the poetical significance of the painting. Many of these inscriptions and seals, however, are apocryphal; in other words, they were added later to express the appreciation of the owner or of an important personage. Consequently it often happens that these additions spoil the perfect visual harmony existing in the original between the painting and the original calligraphic text. Nevertheless, the addition of texts and the application of seals (some of them very beautiful) add to our enjoyment and give the connoisseur yet another proof of the harmony of all the elements forming the whole.

On the other walls of the room there may be two or three mural paintings, or *Chüan*, which the scholar perhaps hung there that very morning, since, like all his contemporaries, he was wont to change them according to his state of mind, or according to the season of the year or the festival falling on that particular day. This is, in fact, an intrinsic characteristic of Chinese mural paintings: they were made to follow the rhythm of change and renewal, in harmony with their owner's state of mind. When a picture was removed from the wall, it was carefully dusted and then rolled up and securely bound with a ribbon.

It may be that our painter keeps his horizontal paintings in an ordinary cupboard. One must examine them slowly as they are unrolled, so that the various scenes follow one upon the other. It might be thought that this gradual manner of looking at a horizontal painting differs considerably from the usual way of looking at a mural painting; but in reality the difference is very slight when we have to deal with a landscape, since a mural painting is also a complex of different visions which should be appreciated separately. Whereas in a painting held in the hand the succession of scenes ensues as we unroll it, in a mural painting it depends on the mounting. It should be noted that in scrolls hung on the wall, the mounting tends to accentuate the top part: in a hung painting the succession of scenes and of points in the landscape begins at the top and gradually descends, as is the case in Chinese writing. In other words, it is possible to read a hung Chinese painting like a page from a book, although the general effect is also of great importance, as it is, indeed, in calligraphy. After some time we notice that our eyes are drawn to the top portion of the painting and that is due not only to the attraction of the mounting, but also to the fact that the seal and the calligraphical text are almost invariably at the top, and in most cases the composition itself draws the eye towards the top. It might legitimately be supposed that this presentation of the scene from different points of view, giving an indefinite and almost unreal effect, is casually due to a certain immaturity in the study of perspective. It is, on the contrary, the mode of expression of artists who thought it essential to present an inner fundamental conception, namely that everything is indefinite and inconstant to

human eyes and that material things as seen by mankind are nothing but illusions. From this attitude springs the ingenious talent of the Chinese artist for endowing the void with the vibrations of air and space, for immerging the twig weighed down by dew into the real atmosphere of a morning or an evening, and for making his peaks and pines float in the fog or the sunset, while remaining invisibly anchored to the ground.

Let us now glance at the sketches which our artist will have made during his wanderings in the open and which lie scattered about on his beautiful table. We shall probably have to answer certain questions: What does he do with them? How does he use them in his work? Probably he uses these aids to his gifted memory as the basis for his calligraphical synthesis and then throws them away. After having, with their help, succeeded in expressing, say, the idea 'grasshopper' with his brush, he destroys all his first attempts, leaving only the last, clear and immutable, for his followers. This explains why no sketches made by the great masters exist. And one of the reasons which lead the neophyte to consider most Chinese paintings as little more than able sketches is that in his calligraphical *résumé* the Chinese painter often achieves extreme simplification.

It should be noted that much of what we have said above refers to the *Shan shui*, those landscape paintings which formed the nucleus of Chinese painting during the last fifteen hundred years. But it would be wrong to think that Chinese painting consists only of landscapes. For the Chinese, portraiture has always been a very important branch of painting, and the very art of painting, as we shall see, began in China with drawings of figures. Nevertheless, although the purely calligraphical style is more used in landscape-painting and the calligraphical origin is therefore clearer in such works, it may be said that this style pervades the whole of Chinese painting. Those who dispute this assertion, point to the figure paintings which existed before landscapes became fashionable (at a time, they say, when calligraphy was already fully developed), as a proof of their contrary opinion. And they base their arguments on the various deviations of painting technique, for example that known as 'spilt-ink', in which, by means of a special technique, the inner form of objects was stressed to the detriment of the outlines. They also maintain that the use of colour, even if rare or hardly used at all in the works of the great masters, is unsuitable to the calligraphical theory. The answer to these critics is that they forget that in calligraphy, too, there were several styles: to mention only one, that which was considered the most suitable for the engraving of seals, which lends itself admirably to the drawing of outlines which could afterwards be filled with colour. On the other hand, the extravagances of Chinese cursive script encourage departures from any kind of orthodoxy.

*

Before discussing the historical development of Chinese painting it will be as well if we forestall the curiosity of the intelligent newcomer as to the great number of Chinese paintings to be found on the market and in Eastern and Western collections. He will be rightly amazed at this superabundance, which is not in conformity with what we said above concerning painting as a form of artistic expression reserved for a limited *élite*. The matter becomes even more puzzling when he is told that enormous quantities of paintings were lost because they formed part of single Imperial collections plundered or burned in the course of wars and rebellions. The truth is that nowadays very few originals of works by the great masters exist. We have only a few copies and many copies of copies, in addition to a large quantity of paintings produced *en masse* for the delectation of Chinese households and a very large number of definitely modern forgeries, complete with texts and seals, and painted on that same paper or silk yellowed by age on which the originals would be if they existed today.

In a preceding chapter we mentioned the Chinese scholar's habit of using the basic concepts of ancient sages which he himself was content merely to elaborate. While no parallel to this assiduous form of dogmatism can be found in history, except perhaps in Catholicism and Marxism, it can easily be discerned in Chinese painting. Since the seventh century at least, generations of Chinese have copied the old masters and copies after the old masters, and that certainly not with the intention of producing forgeries, but with a conscientious and reverent aim. The copies made from the works of these great men were exalted and adorned with laudatory seals, not only because the works were well executed, but also as a reward for the humble respect which such an undertaking implied, just as today a 'comrade' might receive a medal for saying something that had already been said by Lenin. It is hardly necessary to add that there were also innovators, exponents of a new style—men gifted with sufficient strength and greatness to modify what had been handed down to them by tradition. But most Chinese paintings are the work of artists who followed the style of one or the other of the great masters—if they did not actually copy them stroke by stroke. The painter might well say, as for that matter a painter could still say today, 'I follow the style of so-and-so,' in the same spirit in which a modern athlete says, 'I run the 100 yards.'

In time this habit inevitably led to what might seem to be an aberration. About the beginning of the seventeenth century treatises began to appear laying down the rules for reproducing in a painting every imaginable kind of object: birds, trees, mountains, rocks, waterfalls, draperies, the human figure. Even today there are still painters who use these formulae. But if we consider the particular aim of the poet-painter, we shall see that the complete lack of any preoccupation with even the most elementary problems of technical variation gave him a still greater liberty to create poetry through his painting. Something similar, for that matter, has occurred in our own art, where the 'aberration' is in the matter of colour, that everlasting preoccupation of the Western artist, just as poetry was that of the Oriental.

This rigid conformism and the firmly rooted habit of copying the old masters, combined with the incredible talent of the modern Chinese for forgery, are the despair of the connoisseur: the virtuosity required of him borders on the demands of genius. Apart from the fact that he had to have an encyclopaedical knowledge of the field of Chinese painting (an entire world in itself), he must have the specialized intelligence of an expert in detecting forged signatures. He has to make a special study of seals and be constantly armed with the suspicion proper to a police-sergeant. Only in this case can he achieve relative certitude concerning the works of, say, three or four masters.

It is for this reason that honest art-dealers will have nothing to do with 'authentic' Chinese paintings. But that does not prevent a lively trade in other Chinese paintings. If we wish to understand why there is such a great abundance of paintings in China and abroad, we must remember the great popularity enjoyed by pictures in China as embellishments for houses and the Chinese habit of hanging them on the walls in rotation, according to the seasons and the various festivals. Very often a picture was considered on account of its subject to be a kind of mascot, or at all events to have the efficacy of an amulet against evil spirits. To meet the great demand, whole workshops were devoted to the production of paintings *en masse*, as we have already mentioned. The incredible ability peculiar to the Chinese soon enabled the artisans to execute good originals and excellent copies of copies. This production still continues today and anyone who has had the curiosity to study the forgeries on the spot, that is to say in the Peking workshops where most of them are made, will inevitably have felt amazement and admiration for the virtuosity of these men. More than once it has been possible to see the reconstruction of a painting of considerable dimensions from an original fragment no larger than a hand.

No art dealer will ever admit that a competitor is able to find his way through this labyrinth of 'orthodox' copies, of 'originals' produced in series, and of shameless forgeries, until he finally arrives at the authentic originals painted by the great masters. It is even more unlikely, therefore, that he will credit an isolated scholar in a museum or a university with an adequate knowledge in the practical field. It is, for example, very difficult to shake the conviction of an antiquary-salesman that only a very small percentage of the Chinese paintings in Western collections consists of copies made by scholars, or still more unlikely, of authentic originals by the masters to whom they are attributed. Already, however, some modern Western scholars give proof of having penetrated deeply into this very deep sea by declaring that 'the great majority of Chinese paintings to be found on the market and in Eastern and Western collections are mass-produced'. The step from here to a study of the forgeries is rendered more difficult today by the impossibility of studying the forgers, who for that matter are being relentlessly snatched away from their profession by the regulations now in force in the new China.

*

Painting is one of the earliest manifestations of mankind, and it is difficult to establish exactly when it began in the case of a nation whose origins are lost in the darkness of the ages. There are plenty of legends, including fabulous stories of miraculous revelations, often telling of the tortoise and the design on its shell which provided inspiration for its reproduction for divinatory purposes. In any case the first mention of painting in the classics refers to the SHANG-YIN DYNASTY (?1766–1122? B.C.) and, more precisely, to portraits made to honour the Imperial ancestors of a ruler. We have already seen that it is not possible to rely absolutely on these annals, but thanks to archaeological discoveries we know for certain that the bronzes of that period were adorned with stylizations denoting a thorough knowledge of drawing, at least as regards animals. Although the human form does not appear on bronzes before the period of the WARRING STATES (481–221 B.C.), the above-mentioned annals speak of mural paintings already existing in public buildings during the CHOU PERIOD (?1122–221 B.C.) and also describe the subjects: here again portraits, and also the dragon and the tiger, symbols of fertility and readiness. The references in all the later classics, down to the Han Dynasty, likewise speak of mural paintings and of drawings of figures. From all this, and from the first specimens brought to light in the course of excavations, we may conclude that painting as an independent art began in the form of drawings of figures and portraits, the technique used being most probably fresco.

The oldest paintings of which we have direct knowledge belong to the HAN DYNASTY (206 B.C.–A.D. 220), and the most important is undoubtedly the so-called 'Lolang Basket', found in a Korean tomb. Here we see sitting and standing figures, painted on lacquer, arranged so ingeniously that they give the impression of being engaged in animated conversation, and even of conviviality. The inscriptions accompanying each of the personages tell us that they were, so to speak, veritable champions of filial piety. The brushwork is very fine and meticulous; nothing is omitted, not even the rouge on the faces of the women! Obviously, if such a humble object was considered worthy of such artistic care, the mural paintings in the palaces of which the annals speak must have been much more elaborate. In the museum at Boston (Mass.) there are several painted tiles found on Han sites near Loyang, showing male figures and a cockfight. In these, probably because of the very nature of the material, calligraphic brush-strokes are much more in evidence than in the 'Lolang basket'. In conclusion, therefore, we may say that the styles and techniques of Chinese painting were already established by the time of the Han period as regards their essential forms.

Of the historical period that followed the fall of the Hans nothing has been preserved that would allow of direct study. Nevertheless, this period of the THREE KINGDOMS and the SIX DYNASTIES (A.D. 220–589) was perhaps the most important for the development of Chinese painting. It was during these tumultuous times that Buddhism penetrated into China, creating, like a bell that has been struck, sound-waves which provoked reaction and violence and eventually gave a quickening impulse to culture. To this period belong the 'Four Patriarchs' of Chinese painting, of whom the most famous was Ku Kai-Chih. A painting attributed to him, now in the British Museum and illustrating a series of poems grouped under the title 'Admonitions of the Imperial Instructress for the Ladies of the Palace', contains, among other things, the first painted landscape known. It is no exaggeration to say that this painting is a milestone in the history of art. The figures in the foreground may appear to be in the wrong perspective in relation to the panorama, but the fact remains that here we find a little patch of landscape rendered with a sure technique more than a thousand years before anything of the kind appeared in the West. The other scenes of this scroll painting illustrate the tasks assigned to the damsels of the palace, and the graceful poise of the figures reveals an already perfectly developed feeling for composition. The painting is on silk and some of the outlines are filled in with a delicate coral red, others with various shades of brown.

There are whole volumes full of information about this great artist. He began as a painter of Buddhist subjects—an activity considered at that time to be a kind of propaganda and therefore inferior to the work of a State sage. Later, the renaissance of Taoism with its more mundane precepts must have influenced Ku Kai-Chih considerably, for at the end of his life we find him enjoying the reputation of a great eccentric, and, to a certain extent, of a freethinker. Perhaps for this reason, and also on account of the London painting (which remained in the cellars of the museum for years before its value was recognized), he has remained more famous than the other three patriarchs. Nevertheless, Chang Seng-Yu, Lu Tan-Wei and Chan Tzu-Ch'ien were also much admired by their contemporaries. We have evidence that the affection felt by the Chinese for their scholar-painters was not unlike that which the Italians feel for their great singers. The following generations copied the works of the four patriarchs with untiring zeal and diligence throughout the centuries and an infinitesimal part of these copies has come down to us, together with the Ku Kai-Chih in London, which many believe is also a copy. It would seem that all the originals have been destroyed, among them the private collection of 240,000 paintings and calligraphic works which the selfishness of their owner, King Yuan Ti, consigned to the flames in order to prevent their falling into other hands.

The flat technique of drawing used in the carving of the Buddhist bas-reliefs in the Lung Men caves induces us to quote them as examples of the trend of figure-painting during the sixteenth century. There we find a clear presage of the progress achieved by the Sui and T'ang painters with a view to giving life and dignity to their figures by means of an appropriate use of draperies. An even better opportunity of following this development is afforded by another field of study in the Tun Huang caves on the borders of China, on the road leading to Central Asia. This outpost must have been a Buddhist centre of some importance, for it was literally filled with fourth-century temples, which, in the fourteenth century, were adorned with mural paintings. These escaped destruction during the great persecution of Buddhism in the tenth century, but they too were finally destroyed by Tartar raiders. Time and the sand contributed to cause these ruins to be for-gotten, but when they were recently rediscovered, re-mains of frescoes of considerable beauty were found, obviously covering several centuries of evolution. We must not forget, however, that these murals must have been far inferior to those executed by order of the nobles and Emperors to adorn their palaces and the temples of the metropolis. Efforts are still being made to assign a date to these works at Tun Huang, but these have perforce to be cautious, owing to the lack of in-dications giving reliable proof of continuity, unless we are to base ourselves on standardized criteria concern-ing the evolution of styles which might not apply to such a remote and therefore individual field of development.

In the reunified Empire under the SUI DYNASTY (A.D. 589-618), a further development of Buddhism took place. Artists now began to arrive from India and one of the best painters of the period, Wei-Ch'ih Po-Chih-na, as the translation of his name proves, came from abroad, or, to be precise, from Khotan. Nevertheless, religious painting, which by this time had acquired a definite physiognomy, did not achieve its full flowering until the following period, that of the great T'ANG DYNASTY (618–906). From the artistic point of view one is justified in relating these two periods to each other. The first introduced a splendour and a manner (and we have seen how true this was in the field of ceramics) that were to continue into the T'ang period, establishing, during the three hundred years the latter lasted, almost all the styles prevalent during the following ten centuries. Ch'ang An, the capital of T'ang China, became the cultural centre of the whole East. It is in Japan that we can best judge the influence which the painters of this period exercised on the artistic development of neighbouring countries. Even today, for example, Japanese clothing and the mode of arranging the hair is the same as we find in the works of two minor Chinese painters of the early ninth century. One of these two artists exercised his influence through Korea, while in 814 a Buddhist mission brought works by the second to Tokyo, where they are still to be found.

Religious painting, however, was by no means the only, or even the most important, manifestation of art, or during this Golden Age secular painting also flourished in China. We might even say that T'ang painting at the height of its splendour achieved its most typical form in the *genre* known as 'mannerism'. That is also true in the sense that it was during the T'ang period that Chinese painting abandoned its formalism and established its various manners. It could never have achieved such a revolution without liberty of movement, which was more readily conceded to secular than to religious painters. The personalities of the artists began to emerge from their works thanks to their individual mannerisms and interpretations, and some of them even began to sign their works with small and modest seals. Each artist became famous for some speciality. Thus Wu Tao-Tzu (eighth century), who appeared on the scene like a last but vivid ray of light before the twilight of Buddhist painting, became famous as a great painter of religious subjects. The ability of this artist, who flourished exactly in the middle of the T'ang period, was shown in his compositions of figures exalting Buddha, but he also gave something else to Chinese painting, something that was to become an inheritance—space. Wu Tao-Tzu would seem to have achieved this indirectly, by means of a novel audacity of brushwork and by treating the whole picture with a freedom unknown to the meticulous painters who preceded him. This new technique, which he used especially in his landscapes, gave rise to a new trend which, acquiring more and more strength, eventually led to the division of the Chinese school into two different schools: the Northern School, led by Li Ssu-hsün and his son, which carried on with the style of meticulous brushwork, and the Southern School, founded by Wang Wei, who, taking Wu Tao-

PLATE 37. *Bodhisattva* in stone. Sui Dynasty. Height 51¼ inches (130 cm.). *W. R. Nelson Gallery of Art, Kansas City.*

PLATE 38. *Kwanyin* in wood. T'ang Dynasty. Height 6¹/₂ inches (16.5 cm.).
Private Collection, Rome.

PLATE 39. *Bodhisattva* in limestone. T'ang Dynasty. *Collection of Mr. and Mrs. Rockefeller jr., New York.*

PLATE 40. Votive stele in marble, with traces of colour and gilding.
Chili Province. Sung Dynasty. Height 59 inches (150 cm.).
Collection of Ellis Monroe and Jan Kleykamp, New York.

PLATE 41. *Kwanyin* in wood (detail). Sung Dynasty. Height of whole seated figure 31 1/8 inches (79 cm.). *Collection of Sig. Gino Tedeschi, Rome.*

PLATE 42. Figure of a European in glazed earthenware. Ming Dynasty.
Height 8⅞ inches (22.5 cm.). *Private Collection, Rome.*

PLATE 43. Painting on silk, in ink and colour; «The Admonitions of the Imperial Instructress». Part of the horizontal painting entitled «The Bed Scene». Attributed to Ku K'ai Chih (4th century A. D.). Height 7 7/8 inches (20 cm.). *British Museum, London.*

PLATE 44. Painting on silk, in ink. «Summer landscape», by Hsia Kuei. 9 3/4 × 13 inches (25 × 33 cm.). *Private Collection.*

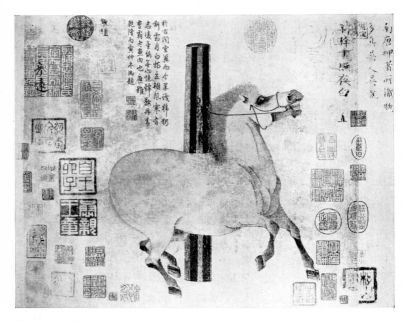

PLATE 45. Painting on paper, in ink with faint colouring. Attributed to Han Kan (8th century A. D.). $12\,^1/_4 \times 13\,^3/_4$ inches (30×35 cm.).
Collection of Sir Percival and Lady David, London.

Tzu's innovations as his starting-point, developed them until he was able to use a painter's bold brushwork to express the purest poetry.

Of the works of the great Wu Tao-tzu, there remain only a few engravings on stone copied from paintings by his hand. It is said that he executed as many as three hundred frescoes in Ch'ang An and Loyang alone, as well as an enormous quantity of horizontal paintings and calligraphical works. But the experts and collectors tell us that almost all his works had already disappeared two hundred years after his death. The T'ang Dynasty ended with a bout of persecution of Buddhism—the religion which was gradually acquiring political power. Almost all the Buddhist temples were destroyed and along with them Wu Tao-tzu's paintings and frescoes.

There are naturally plenty of fables and legends about this painter, who is considered one of the greatest China has ever had. One of them, particularly amusing, tells how he left this earth through one of his own paintings. More reliable is the written evidence, which informs us that Wu Tao-tzu was one of the few professional painters; in other words, he was neither a scholar nor a civil servant, although in his last years he may have been appointed to some minor sinecure post.

Another great artist of this great period was Han Kan, a painter of horses. Together with his colleague Chang Hsüan, a painter of women, he worked in the palace for the Emperor Ming Huang (712–756), who loved horses as much as he did women. Unfortunately, hardly anything remains of their works, but the beautiful little figures of horses and women found in T'ang tombs give us an idea of the magnificent and elegant works that these Court painters must have been able to produce for their monarch.

Yen Li-pen (seventh century) was another artist who contributed greatly to the extension of the limits of painting and to that affirmation of individuality which makes the T'ang painters the founders of a new canon. A high civil servant and a great scholar, as a painter he specialized in portraits of historical personages and he knew how to heighten the personality of his sitters and to make more effective use of colour, thus contributing to a better knowledge of this medium. His brother-in-law, Yen Li-tze, was also a well-known painter, who specialized in portraits.

Towards the end of the T'ang Dynasty there were other deviations. The painting of small natural objects —birds, flowers, insects—which hitherto had had purely decorative aims, became an aim in itself. The school of South-Western China, probably founded by Huang Chüan, who took refuge there after the disintegration of the T'ang regime, established a style which still influences the painting of today—that of treating birds and flowers as if they were sacred.

The stage was now set for the advance that painting was to make during the following period. But before the complete extinction of the T'angs another painter appeared, who in his turn was destined to exercise a great influence on the following generation—the Buddhist priest Kuan-hsiu (832–912). He painted Lohans, endowing them with a strange expressionistic vitality, stressing the emaciated bodies and giving them an exotic and sometimes almost ferocious aspect. His sincerity and his fervour lend strength and dignity to the Lohans he painted. Until quite recent times these curious characters of his have been copied, in the production of little monsters not only on paper, but also in ivory, porcelain and wood; of them the best that can be said is that they are useful as necessary counterparts to beauty.

*

The fifty-three years of the FIVE DYNASTIES (A.D. 907–960) were destined to pass before the remnants of the great T'angs could once more be reunited under a Chinese government. From the point of view of painting, this interlude must be considered as a period of transition from the virile and warlike manner of the T'angs to the enlightened refinement of the SUNG DYNASTY (960–1279).

A brief historico-religious digression will help to explain the nature of this period. Buddhism, opposed by a tolerant race because of its infiltrations into the political structure of the country, had undergone a radical change. Nevertheless, the violence of the persecutions had deeper roots in a peculiarity of the Chinese people—their basic rationalism. Irritated and offended at first by the ritualistic and grotesque trend which the pure doctrines of Buddha assumed thanks to the work of foreign propagandists, the populace rebelled, but later allowed the importation from India of another brand of the same religion, the *Ch'an* (contemplation) form, a treasury of lofty thoughts. The importance of this deviation cannot be exaggerated, and nor can the great satisfaction the new religious form (which still has many adherents today in Japan, where it is known as Zen Buddhism) brought to the enlightened group which in China practised the arts. It is sufficient to say that this dissenting sect became fused with Taoism and that in this congenial spiritual trend even doctrinary Confucianism eventually found an outlet.

The credit for this happy result must be given to the ability of the Sung scholars. Even though Marco Polo's visit to China took place several years later, no description of the state of the Empire at that time could be more complete than that found in his writings, for the way of life was still that of the Sungs. His description of Hangchow, the Sung capital after their long flight before the Mongol invaders, agrees perfectly with what we read in the Chinese annals of those times. We can only conclude that this period, which had inherited the magnificence of the T'angs and knew how to change it into elegance, must have been an epoch perhaps unique in the history of the world for its splendour and harmony. The erudite functionaries, whom the Han Emperors had compelled to take examinations in order that they might be kept under control, in time learned how to use them as a means of controlling the Emperor. The actual government was now in their hands. They eventually succeeded in organizing life according to a peaceful system of prosperity for all, and from such serenity art could easily spring—serene, gentle, varied, a perfect mirror of the times. Like Taoism, Ch'an Buddhism taught that Divinity is everywhere, that Reality can be found in the stem of a flower as it can in the intimate mind of a man, that everything deserves to be worshipped and that histrionic ritualistic forms must be shunned. A mystical and animistic urge accompanied the visions of the painters, and the 'vibrant space' ('the great void' according to Ch'an terminology) formed the most durable contribution made by these neo-Buddhist artists. Colour was abandoned in order to give free rein to Intuition, because 'colour is illusion, and illusion is colour'. Paintings were executed with great speed, the artist's hand was seized by a feverish anxiety. At no time had calligraphy been closer to painting than now. Through the man and his calligraphy, a natural force expressed something of what it had created. The mediator, the sifter, the painter had to keep himself pure, conceding nothing to the body and listening to the spirit through the practice of meditation.

*

It would nevertheless be wrong to suppose that this new Buddhist manner had an absolute influence, and still more so to consider the Ch'an manner, which was of foreign inspiration, as being the same as religion itself. Since, with the advent of the Sung Dynasty, all foreign influences had been absorbed and transformed, we can say that this dynasty offers us the first mature, modern and purely Chinese expression in painting.

Art, one might say, was officially recognized by the government. The Emperor Tai Tsung (976–997) founded the first Academy of Painting, which, to a far greater extent than any other cultural organization, became a kind of ministry. One of the members of this Academy was the great painter and teacher Kuo Hsi (eleventh century). With the help of his son he laid down fixed rules for painting, and some of these, in verse, were later meditated upon and often learned by heart by his industrious followers. It was at this time that calligraphic poetry became a normal adjunct to pictures and that the two forms of art were definitely fused. Intellectual *coteries* flourished in the Academy *milieu*. Styles, manners and trends were refined by means of discussion—discussions which were concerned not only with painting, but also with poetry, affairs of State and philosophy.

The head of one of these groups was Mi Fei (?1051–1107), a friend of the artist and radical reformer Wang An-Shih and of the great poet Su Tung-Po. An obstinate and arrogant man, he was not afraid to criticize the Academy, the Emperor's creation, and he did all he could to encourage a tendency to secede from that institution, which he considered to be too attached to formalism and dogma. Naturally, this attitude brought him little success in his political career, but his personal charm must have been considerable and his sincerity obvious. He maintained (and his friends agreed with him) that paintings ought not to be shown to everybody, and that it is as difficult to understand a work of art as it is to create it. His contribution to art was the invention of the 'dot' which bears his name, that is to say, the method of rendering masses by little dots which allow the light to filter through. Many centuries later Seurat created the same effect of light by using little dots of colour.

The pictorial representation of the bamboo brought about a closer harmony between calligraphy and painting. Wen Tung (?1041–1079), a member of Mi Fei's group, was the greatest of these painters. He died young, to the great grief of his friends, but his fame still endures. There is a subtle element in this peculiar specialization in one subject, something elusive that defies all explanation. The bamboo plant in itself is a veritable symposium of qualities—from the softness of its tender buds to the pointed elegance of the leaves, from the stiffness of each of its tubular segments to the sinuosity of the whole branch. The driving wind imparts a paean of movement to the plant. To contrive to render lightly these diverse states of mind, with a hand no less passionate than the elements themselves, requires love rather than skill. Other plants which were the object of like devotion were the blossoming briar, the chrysanthemum and the orchid, which, together with the bamboo, were known to the Chinese as the 'Four Gentlemen'. Hordes of Chinese painters tried their skill in rendering these basic themes, just as hordes of Chinese actors practised their art in the three or four dramas constituting the whole of the classical repertory.

Li Lung-Mien (1040–1106) was another friend of Mi Fei and member of his group, the close union of which it is difficult for Westerners to understand, since they are accustomed to see more antagonism than anything else in every artistic community. Li was perhaps the best painter of them all and certainly the most versatile. His manner was as limpid and fluid as water and he possessed the gift of knowing how to identify himself with the subject he was painting, to such an extent that his friends used to dissuade him from depicting horses, for fear lest he might become a horse himself! He must have been a very sociable man, for it was to him that the Chinese owe the habit of several painters working together on one picture. One of his works, representing scholars on one of the excursions during which it was the custom to put this collaboration into practice, found an incredible number of zealous copyists.

A short time before the Sung Dynasty was compelled to migrate to the South, the Emperor Hui Tsung (1101–1125), himself an artist, compiled and published a minutely classified catalogue, including an examination in the art of painting among those which candidates for government posts had to pass. But the artists of his own time paid little attention to his pedantically meticulous classifications and continued to give free expression to their own fancies.

During the second phase of the Sung Dynasty, the so-called 'Southern Sung', the refinement and subtleness of painting reached its zenith. A flair for elegant allusions became an essential quality for every self-respecting painter. All emphasis was despised and when the Emperor asked his painters to illustrate the lines:

I return from trampling upon flowers
And the hooves of my horse smell sweet,

the prize was awarded to the author of a picture showing two butterflies hovering round a horse's hoofs.

In this atmosphere of subtle search for the exquisite, the great school of Chinese landscape-painting came to full flower. From that time on landscape-painting might well be called 'classic'. The literary game of the butterfly around the hoof is extended to the solution of purely pictorial problems in a subtly simple manner in which the aim is to say as much as possible with as little as possible. For the spectator, the mental effort required in order to grasp the meaning of a painting becomes greater and greater. Emptiness, space, now vibrate. The painter Ma Yüan (twelfth to thirteenth centuries) produced his lonely fishermen and his mighty pine-trees defying all conventional arrangements. Since he was a member of the Academy, his work was meticulous where it could be seen, but in his silences, in his empty expanses of water and sky he was a veritable revolutionary. The same academic conscience is discernible in the works of Hsia Kuei, the other great master of this period. But when dense foliage obscures his skies or his tree-trunks are swayed and battered by the tempest, his pulse quickens spasmodically and his calligraphy becomes almost frantic. During the whole of their lives these two masters contrived to permeate the Academy with their originality. It appears that during this period another painter, Liang Kai, was expelled on account of his passion for innovation. His paintings (or rather, the copies of his paintings that have come down to us) reveal two completely different styles. In the course of his evolution, he achieved a simplification that must be considered the ultimate in the art, but his brushwork remains so powerful and concentrated that his figures palpitate with life. The Sung Dynasty, that great period of Chinese art, thus ended by achieving the acme of inventiveness, individuality and refinement. Though still virile, the art of painting was ripe for further evolution.

*

And this evolution took place with the advent of the invader Kublai, who swept away everything he found before him, including the ephemeral Chin Tartars, and established himself in Peking under the style of YUAN (1280–1368). After the passage of so many centuries and from the point of view which interests us, namely that of painting, we might say that the most salient characteristic of this Mongol barbarian was his adaptability. Having rebuilt the city which he himself had destroyed, he made it his capital and adopted with the greatest ease the system followed by his Sung predecessors. The scholars were invited to Court, painting was placed under his personal protection; the first painter to enter the palace, in 1286, was Chao Meng-fu, and thereafter a veritable *coterie* of artists gradually began to frequent the Court.

It was a time of change, the time to return—as a homage to a man of action—to the vigorous manner of the T'ang painters, to exploit with renewed zeal their predilection for horses—a predilection very much to the taste of a nomad. Two famous painters who followed Chao Meng-fu and devoted themselves to the painting of horses were Jen Jen-Fa and Kung K'ai, though it is said that the latter refused an invitation from the Emperor to enter the palace. This trio of painters was outstanding for a new and robustly explicit manner, despite the fact that the chroniclers of that time were obsessed with the beloved wife of Chao Meng-Fu, whose life would seem to have been fuller and more intense than that of any classical personage. Besides being the mother of nine children, Lady Kuan Tao-shen was the greatest woman painter China has ever had and authoress of a treatise on painting the bamboo which is still a textbook today. Moreover, according to her husband, she was also the best of daughters, wives and mothers, and, according to a Court historian, a kind of Chinese Madame de Sévigné in the Mongol's palace. From all this and other sources of information concerning the women painters of the time, we can deduce that women were once again taking part in the intellectual life of the country, as they had already done under the T'angs.

A form of painting handed down directly from the Sungs, which was considerably developed during the Yuan Dynasty and achieved a great vogue, was that of rendering the bamboo. It received a great impulse from the works of painters like Ku An and Li K'an, the latter being considered a prince in this particular *genre*. According to certain modern scholars, the artists of that time considered the bamboo as a symbol of China, battered by the wind of the caprices of a barbarian government. But perhaps the vogue of the bamboo was nothing but the natural consequence of a recent and very fertile discovery, namely the calligraphic pleasure to be derived from the painting of such a plant. The secret of this kind of painting lies in knowing how to handle the brush with a swift power and intensity; it really seems as if Ch'an painting had finally overstepped its bounds.

Towards the end of the brief Yuan Dynasty, the tendency to reproduce things exactly as they are seen appears so suddenly as to make us suspect a first infiltration of Western influences. But on the other hand other purely Chinese characteristics grew stronger. Calligraphical poems now form part of the works of the great landscape-painters of the time: Huang Kung-Wang, Wu Chen, Ni Tsan and Wang Men, known as the 'Four Masters'. They introduced elements which were to make Ming Baroque more acceptable. For all their simplicity, their works reveal, on the whole, a certain desire to *épater*—though this might seem to be an almost blasphemous observation, since these austere and lonely men were exalted for their honesty and for the independence they showed in their dealings with the Khan's Court.

*

The four masters we have just mentioned lived on into the following MING DYNASTY (1368–1644) and were greatly revered and zealously imitated. But the novice will rightly expect us to give him some general information, so that he can obtain a notion of this period, which in other fields witnessed the last emanations of Chinese artistic genius.

The truth is that the efforts made by the conquerors to return to their favourite T'ang prototypes had little success in painting. Recently, there have been attempts to overstress the value of the painting of this Dynasty by giving the artists the same importance that they were given by the Chinese. This, however, would be an obvious exaggeration—if for no other reason because this Dynasty offers us nothing which is really original.

Scholars find themselves confronted with a great confusion of 'schools', which, once disentangled, reveals only one fact, namely that after the change in the whole social structure of the Empire and the appearance of a middle class, there was a schism in the ranks of the painters. The amateurs, so to speak, the *literati* who painted merely for love of art, retired behind the screen of a school, 'the School of the Scholars', thus leaving in isolation the category of professionals which had in the meantime emerged. After a first forcible intervention in the affairs of the country, the Emperors took a period of rest, during which they showed a keen interest in the *literati*. New schools were formed, some of them assuming the by now recognized names of 'Southern' and 'Northern', but such differentiations no longer had any geographical basis, nor any logical explanation. Women still took part in intellectual life: in the artistic history of China, Wen-Shu (1595–1634) is second only to Lady Kuan Tao-Sheng. She painted whole albums of flowers and insects. Birds and animals, the favourite subjects of Ming painters, were executed with the greatest competence, though sometimes in a rather decorative manner. We do, however, find paintings of animals revealing an almost miraculous talent: these are sometimes of unknown species, their terrifying glance reminding us of the *Tao-tieh* of the Shangs and Chous.

There was a return to the drawing of figures in the T'ang manner. But painters now endowed their personages with a noteworthy brilliance of colouring and increased the dimensions of their pictures. Frescoes abounded in the pavilions of the Imperial palaces and in the halls of temples. The chauvinist-minded Dynasty rejected the foreign religion of Buddhism and drew nearer and nearer to Confucius.

There were, nevertheless, painters of talent deserving of mention. Shen Chou (1427–1509) was a real poet of the brush, while Tai Chin, his contemporary, was colder, but not lacking in nobility. Both were landscape-painters, though they show more interest in figures than their predecessors, introducing more of them to give animation to their pictures. These two painters were definitely superior to their contemporaries, but, perhaps because he was a professional, the merits of Tai Chin were not appreciated until after his death.

Another good landscape-painter of the seventeenth

century was T'ang Yin. His style had considerable influence on the Japanese prints of subsequent periods, and this merit is also due to his brother Ching Ying, who executed innumerable paintings with the collaboration of almost the whole of his family.

*

This was also the era of mass-copying. The scholars won their brief struggle with the professionals and retired into their citadel of culture, repeating again and again what only they knew. They painted, wrote about painting, criticized and formulated rules. They had by now become crystallized and were no longer capable of creating.

But the great art of this ancient people was not destined to die out in this way. At the very end of the Ming Dynasty a new group of artists appeared, among them Hsiang Sheng-Mo (1597–1658), known to us above all for the magnificent horizontal painting now in the Royal Ontario Museum. With these young men the Dynasty came to an end, but they were the harbingers of an imminent prodigy.

*

The CH'ING DYNASTY (1644–1911), established by the Manchu invaders who intervened to help a Chinese general usurp the throne, proved to be more eager even than the Mongol Yuans to adopt Chinese customs. Their second Emperor, the great K'ang Hsi (1662–1722), spent the sixty years of his reign fusing the Manchu form of government with Chinese methods, and we must admit that he was extremely successful.

By the time he died, the Manchu rulers had become more Chinese than their subjects—in their respect for ancestral traditions, their obedience to the laws of Confucian ethics and their love of art. Under this Emperor (himself a painter) the great enterprise was begun of compiling gigantic Imperial encyclopaedias, catalogues and inventories. Conformity with the past became so essential that an artist could not call himself a painter unless he had first compiled an anthology of the old masters in at least fifty volumes. The *literati* still had the upper hand and unfortunately their close study of earlier painters is revealed in their works. By an error of judgement these learned men succumbed to a strong liking for Yuan painting. Actually, the famous 'Four Wangs' did contribute something new to painting by making an accurate study of mountain crevices, but they later became rather monotonous, repeating themselves time after time. They were, however, highly esteemed by their contemporaries and were anxious to impart their knowledge to others. The newly enriched middle class bought their paintings, while the Court commissioned them to execute important decorations in the palace. Two of them, Wang Hui (1632–1720) and Wang Yüan-chih, worked under the direct orders of K'ang Hsi. The former knew how to lend a romantic atmosphere to his paintings, animating the landscape with tiny houses and thoughtful wayfarers, while the latter's exaggeratedly meticulous work reveals his anxiety not to depart from academical precepts. Nevertheless, the figure of this man stands out among the unmercenary Chinese scholars, because of a peculiar characteristic: he was very greedy for money and seems to have spent as much time haggling in the hope of getting better prices for his works as he did in compiling encyclopaedias and painting. Notwithstanding this, his fame still endures among the Chinese of today.

Another painter who had a very peculiar personality was Wu Li (1643–1708). It would seem that after becoming a Jesuit (!), he travelled a great deal in Europe. But his works are notable only for a certain boldness in the conception of the landscapes, possibly due to Western influences.

Women still continued to paint, and successfully. They devoted themselves with all seriousness to painting with the fingers, an agreeable pastime which from time to time became fashionable in the course of the centuries. But we must look elsewhere for the real original artists of this period. They were not to be found at the Court, nor in the studies of the scholars, and not even in the *atelier* of the greedy Wang, who had a whole troop of assistants under his command. The prodigies, of whom the last Ming painters were the forerunners, were monks, Ch'an Buddhist monks who worked in their hermitages, far from the Court of the barbarian whom they despised.

Never before had there been so much individualism and so much iconoclasm in Chinese art. These men openly declared that copying the old masters meant stagnation and with the greatest simplicity drew attention to the fact that the best way to paint is not to follow anyone. The powerful contemplative expressiveness thereby achieved, obtained with only a few strokes of the brush and the use of very little ink, is particularly worthy of note in the works of Chu Ta (1626–1705). The urge to rebel against the new order also led these monks to rebel against the old order. Their move-

PLATE 46. Painting on silk, in colour. Tree, peony and pheasants, by Wang Hu. Ming Dynasty. Height 69 inches (175 cm). *British Museum, London.*

PLATE 47. Painting on silk, in ink. «Sleeping in a Boat near the Bank». Attributed to Kung K'ai. Sung Dynasty. Height 40½ inches (103 cm). *Freer Gallery of Art, Washington.*

PLATE 48. Painting on silk, in ink and faint colour. «Landscape and Sage».
In the manner of Ma Yüan. Sung Dynasty. Height 74 inches (188 cm.).
Freer Gallery of Art, Washington.

PLATE 49. Painting on silk, in ink. «Bamboo buds», by Wu Chen.
Yuan Dynasty. $8^5/_8 \times 8^1/_2$ inches (22×21.5 cm.).
Eumorfopulos Collection, British Museum, London.

PLATE 50. Painting on silk, in ink and colour. «Animals», by an unknown artist. Ming Dynasty. Height 70 inches (178 cm.).
Collection of Sig. Arnaldo Camporelli, Milan.

PLATE 51. Painting on silk, in colour (detail). «The Hundred Horses Grazing»,
by Giuseppe Castiglione (Lang Shih Ning). Chien Lung period.
Chinese Government.

PLATE 52. Painting on silk, in colour. « Ts'ui Yung-yin with her lover », by an unknown artist. Chien Lung period. Height 76³/₄ inches (195 cm.).
Freer Gallery of Art, Washington.

PLATE 53. Taoist sage, in ivory. Ming Dynasty. Height 3 1/2 inches (10 cm.).
Collection of Avvocato Luigi d'Amelia, Rome.

PLATE 54. Immortal, in ivory. Ming Dynasty. Height $4^7/_8$ inches (12.5 cm.). *Collection of the S. & G. Gump Company, San Francisco.*

ment was political and the play of calligraphy in their paintings and even their seals were pregnant with non-conformist allusions. Shih-t'ao's little paintings of flowers, bamboos and birds bear the hallmark of genius. K'un-Ts'an, on the other hand, painted landscapes so terrifying and wild that we are compelled to ask ourselves whether he derived them from his dreams. All these monks, however, showed a disconcerting skill in combining reality with illusion, so that it is often difficult to distinguish the two. The strength of rebellion shines out from their works—a last glimmer of that marvellous fire that had burned for at least three thousand years.

*

We cannot refrain from mentioning here the Jesuit Fathers who came to China and became painters at the Ch'ing Court, since it is to them that Chinese painting owes its last evolution, namely the trend towards the West which even today has not yet become stabilized. One of them, the Italian Giuseppe Castiglione (active from 1715 to 1766), became a great favourite of the Emperor and at the end of his long and prosperous career was honoured in a way bordering on veneration. After beginning his career under the great Emperor K'ang Hsi, he worked for Yung Cheng and finally for Chien Lung. The reason for his success at Court, far greater than that of his *confrères* (Attiret and Sichel-barth, among others), was that he preferred to let himself be influenced by the Chinese manner rather than to impose his own. His paintings can be dated on the basis of the various styles he employed. He began by painting portraits in oil in the Italian manner of the early eighteenth century and ended by producing horizontal paintings of horses moving across boundless landscapes. There is nothing foreign in these paintings except the roundness of the trees and of the horses' bellies, but the compromise made by this Jesuit Father had a considerable influence on Chinese painters. Even today there are two or three scholar-painters living in Peking who execute paintings of this kind with such perfection that they can sell them, or have them sold, as authentic works by Lang-Shih-Ning (the Italian Jesuit's Chinese name).

Castiglione's first manner, and that of his *confrères* who remained more faithful to Europe than he did, also had considerable influence. In the eighteenth and nineteenth centuries we find portraits in oil and tempera of beautiful women and venerable mandarins which might easily have been executed by mediocre, but elegant, Italian or French painters.

We have unfortunately now come to the definite eclipse of Chinese painting and there is as yet no sign of the coming of a real renaissance. Art has met with the same fate as all those other Chinese institutions consecrated by age: they have not yet found a way of resisting the impact of Western influence, and still less of reacting to it.

Yet in the four thousand years of history, according to the Chinese system of counting time by centuries, the present age and the two or three hundred years preceding it are practically nothing, merely another period of transition. The Chinese are waiting. And we have the best of historical and scientific reasons for waiting too.

CHAPTER SEVEN

The Ivories

THE first mention of ivory in the Chinese classics is very ancient. During a golden age of erudition and philosophy, coinciding roughly with the Graeco-Persian wars, a Chinese scholar, with a carefulness which proves how anxious he was to be understood by posterity, mentions the fact that ivory was considered very valuable and was accepted by the Court in payment of taxes and tributes. The above-mentioned scholar then adds a personal observation, to the effect that the value of ivory as a material will probably prove fatal to the elephant and concludes by deploring that so powerful and noble an animal has such inadequate means of defending itself against the pitiless greed of mankind. Two hundred years later we learn from another historian that a certain minister tried to gain favour with his prince by presenting him with an ivory bed, and, at a still later period, that dignitaries were in the habit of wearing with pride and reverence ivory tablets denoting their rank at Court. A more mundane man of letters expatiates on the more frivolous uses to which the precious tusks were put: 'The courtesans dip their slender fingers in ivory boxes containing perfumed cosmetics; the gourmets carry with them their own little ivory sticks for eating rice and the new rich hang their hats on ivory hatstands, while men of the world admire their favourite crickets through the delicate fretwork of ivory forming the lids of the special boxes carved out of gourds. I myself have bought a tiny bridge of ivory on which I rest my wrist while writing.'

Archaeology, however, takes a more profound, even if less refined, view. The decorations on the Anyang bronzes of the SHANG-YIN DYNASTY (?1766–1122? B.C.) prove conclusively that the elephant was used as a motive, thus showing that the primitive inhabitants of the Huang Ho valley were familiar with this animal. The discovery of ivory fossils allows us to go even further back and to conclude that the elephant (and probably its mastodontic predecessors as well) roamed the Chinese plains from the remotest times; but we do not know when exactly it ceased to form part of the Chinese fauna. One of China's most ancient relics is an incised piece of ivory shaped like a horned *tao-tieh*—the ubiquitous decorative element we have already discussed in the chapter on the bronzes. This was found in the valley of the Yellow River and is attributed to a period ranging from 1500 to 1000 B.C. If, therefore, ivory was used as a precious material for ritual ornaments in such remote times we are justified in supposing that the remark about human greed made by the scholar of the 'Tso Chwan' must have been correct, at least as far as Chinese elephants were concerned.

Once the Chinese supplies of ivory had been exhausted, the leading merchants financed caravans for the transport of tusks from Burma and India, and later, even from Africa. Much study and skill are required before one is in a position to judge the quality of ivory. Its value depended not only on the size of the tusk (important in any case since an article made out of one piece could be sold at a price far higher than that calculated on mere weight), but also on the grain, the colour and the brilliance. From the earliest times African ivory was considered the best, but other factors often outweighed this purely geographical element. It was most important to know whether the tusk came from an animal that had been killed (a decidedly positive factor), or from one that had died a natural death, and in the latter case how much time had elapsed between death and the finding of the ivory. These considerations had a noteworthy influence on the prices, and for that matter this is still true of our own days, the trade in ivory being now in the hands of very distinguished gentlemen who sit in dark and very clean, wainscoted shops. This, at all events, is what we see in the most accessible parts of modern China, such as Taiwan, Hong Kong and Macao, where the trade is still held in great respect.

In the early days only the Imperial families could afford the luxury of using such a valuable material. It was they who encouraged the art of carving on ivory, just as they had encouraged the manufacture of porcelain, carving on jade and the creation of fabrics and tapestries. Workshop-schools founded by the Court under the Sung Dynasty (A.D. 960–1279) made ornaments for personal use and small articles of furniture for the palace. Some of these reveal a high degree of inventive skill and great ability on the part of their makers.

But it was the work of other men that was to obtain for ivory the designation of 'art' in the most literal sense of the word.

*

Aware of his own significance, as the result of the philosophical and religious teaching he had received, and convinced that he was merely an ordinary link in the chain in the Confucian system of the eternal family, the Chinese artist rarely thought fit to assert his own immortal individuality by affixing his signature to his works. If he signed his paintings, it was only in order to make clear their artistic origin, just as the owners asserted their ownership and the admirers their admiration by placing their signatures afterwards on the paintings. More important, infinitely more important for the artist, was his ability to render the state of mind of the individual and his humanity, the conceptions and the philosophical point of view of a human being. If the work was incapable of revealing all this, the inscription added to the painting by the artist came to the rescue. Existence, thought and feeling have always been the three great mysteries in the presence of which the Chinese feel surprise and reverence. And this attitude inevitably leads to the elimination of all personal exhibitionism.

The exact, or even approximate, authorship of the works we are about to examine must thus remain a mystery. So far as we know, no signed works in ivory exist, and as a general rule any signatures found on ivory carvings of any period must be attributed to Japanese artists.

The mystery enveloping these exquisite works is rendered even deeper by the lack of any reference to them in Chinese literature. A careful examination of the objects is thus the only way to discover their identity, or at least to estimate their value. And the temptation to attribute a religious sentiment to the men who executed these wonderful works, the so-called Ming ivories, is so strong in the author that he feels it incumbent upon him to make a theory out of a hypothesis.

At a time when the artist was little more than an ordinary artisan engaged in perfecting the technical possibilities of materials that had already been artistically exploited during the preceding Sung period, it is in the field of ivories alone that we find this process reversed. The material, precious though it was, had been used in the past (and was destined to be used in the future) by men whom we call artisans, but at this time it suddenly became the medium for another form of sculpture. It was found that ivory was the ideal medium for small statues destined to be used as ornaments for altars, and the religious fervour of a group of artisans contrived to endow their works with a sincerity, a profundity and an expressive force that can bear comparison with the greatest masterpieces of religious art. The flamboyant Renaissance Christ was the work of a pious humanist; the Immortal reproduced in Plate 54 is the work of a contemplative and mystical Oriental.

But how did this sculptor-monk of the MING DYNASTY (1368–1644) obtain his artistic training and where can he have found the models for his creations? The student of Chinese art can easily reply to these questions. The little T'ang figures in earthenware, placed in the tombs beside the dead, can be considered as the forerunners of these new carvings on ivory. It was from them that the monk took the expressive movement of the draperies, the serene charm of the attitudes. But the qualities that raised the Ming statuettes to the status of an art were also derived from the

Buddhist caves at Lung Men, Yung-k'an and Tien-lung-shan, and perhaps from another more elusive source which it is difficult to define. To the innumerable elements of clay and stone it was man, and man alone, who gave a finished form; but ivory derives its form, its grain, colour and texture from a process of growth, from an organization which transcends the human hand. The merit of the Ming religious ivory-carvers lies precisely in the fact that they left this extraordinary dimension intact, this, for them, immediate revelation of a supernatural force. Their carvings invariably follow the first organic scheme decreed by God, and they do everything possible to avoid departing from it. The Ming statuette is thus an instrument provided with an additional chord; it seems almost as if the artist has endowed it with a moment of eternity, like that which vibrates in the absolute void of one of Ma Yuan's skies.

Of course, there are other elements in these ivory carvings which distinguish them from the T'ang figurines and the Lung Men sculptures. Whereas the stone statues in the caves were the work of a sect that derived a new strength from suffering and persecution, the little Ming ivories reveal the religious serenity of a happy group. Sometimes, almost jestingly, the artist uses the grain of his material to stress a particular point, to reproduce the wrinkled skin of one of his Lohans. At other times, he exploits the curve of the tusk in order to give greater relief to the sinuous grace of a girl. There are very few pieces which do not reveal the intelligent skill of an artist who inevitably must also have been a portraitist. For in this, too, his work differs from the stone statues of the preceding periods: except

PLATE 55. Small model for use by a physician, in ivory. Ming Dynasty. Height 4 7/8 inches (12.5 cm.).
Collection of Principessa Pallavicini, Rome.

PLATE 56. Jade mask of a human face. Shang-Yin Dynasty. Height $1^3/_4$ inches (4.5 cm.). *W. R. Nelson Gallery of Art, Kansas City.*

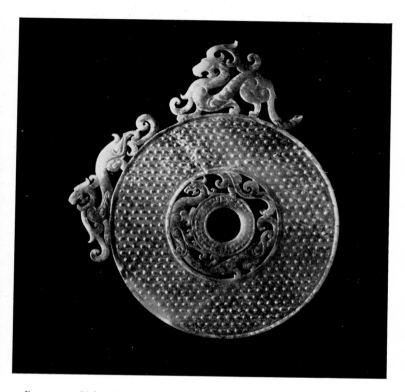

PLATE 57. *Pi* in white jade. Early Chou Dynasty. Diameter of the disc 6¹/₂ inches (16.5 cm.). *W. R. Nelson Gallery of Art, Kansas City.*

PLATE 58. Head of a horse, in green jade. Han Dynasty. *Eumorfopulos Collection, Victoria & Albert Museum, London.*

when he undertakes to portray the traditional personages of his pantheon—Kwan Yin, dispenser of charity;
the Eight Immortals; the divine Buddha—he allows
himself so much liberty as regards the minor deities
that he achieves a notable variety of types, inspired,
very probably, by living models (Plate 53).

One likes to imagine that these devout artists also
devoted their talents to more mundane works. In the
little recumbent figure reproduced in Plate 55, the
carver certainly did not intend to render the amusing
or tantalizing aspects of an unclothed and rather plump
woman. And if he has nevertheless achieved this result,
it is because a true artist cannot work with any material
without giving it life. The aim of these little figures
was, in actual fact, scientific, for they were used by
physicians, who produced them from their pockets in
the presence of their patients, so that the latter might
indicate the exact point where they felt pain. It is
obvious that among the Chinese belief in the purely
scientific attitude of doctors never attained the same
high level that it did in the West. And this leads us to
an interesting reflection on the nude as a source of
artistic inspiration. The Chinese prefer to ignore nudity
and the reactions it may arouse in the spectator, as they
never make any allusion to the appetites of other kinds
with which Nature has endowed us. For the Chinese,
the assertion that nudity is beauty might, at the very
most, be considered as a very ephemeral truth, and
every attempt to exploit its artistic possibilities is
viewed by them with suspicion.

It would seem, however, that science provided China
with the excuse which elsewhere was provided by
aesthetic reasons, for these 'diagnostic ivories' must

have enjoyed considerable popularity in their time. Many of these little statues have come down to us, but so far as we know, none of them was found in a tomb. The majority appear to lack the extremities and it is believed that in the following periods, owing to the memory of the connection between these figures and medical practice, ignorant laymen ground the ivory to a fine powder and used it as a medicine. For that matter, this is a practice which was still followed until a few years ago in the province of Hopei, where the chemists used to sell ground ivory as a panacea for all ills.

The attribution of these beautiful carvings, whether sacred or profane, to the Ming Dynasty has for some time been an established fact, on which we may, in the main, rely. But it is difficult to be more exact, in other words to establish a more detailed chronology covering the 276 years of the Dynasty. It is believed that many of them date from the last years of the Ming period, and we may therefore assume that some of them were still being produced under the Ch'ing Dynasty. The works of the K'ang Hsi period reveal a pictorial striving typical of this period and of the reigns of Yung Chen and Chien Lung, but in the expressiveness of the types they preserve the Ming quality which was later lost.

From the end of the K'ang Hsi onwards, ivory is left to the artisans. Figures for the adornment of elaborate screens were still carved, but for the most part they are flat and almost bi-dimensional. Tiny ivory screens were also made to add lustre to the desks of literary men, and also *pi-tong*, round bowls carved out of the hollow roots of big tusks, in which the writer placed his brushes for writing and painting. The first *pi-tong* have no decorations, but during the last years of the Ming period and the first of the Ch'ing they are elegantly incised and show garden scenes, religious processions and landscapes.

At the turn of the century, however, the Empress Mother Tzu Shih, as imperious in her bad taste as she was in everything else, commanded that portraits of herself be made in ivory and required her furniture-dealers to supply her with armchairs having the colour and the rough texture of elephant's skin, with real ivory tusks as arm-rests. The age of beauty has gone. The Chinese love for grain and warmth of materials is no more. Many, too many, statuettes are still produced today. Stiff and hard, they are quite white, unless they are first soaked in tea or smoked like hams in order to deceive the purchaser, or—even worse—painted in blue, green and red to make them strike the eye. The days when there was poetry in materials have definitely vanished.

In the study of the lonely scholar there still lingers a faint echo of the poet's eulogy: '. . . For ivory is a beautiful material: it is the elephant's generous excuse for his clumsiness and, at the same time, the swordpoint of his strength.'

CHAPTER EIGHT
Jade

THE great reverence the Chinese have always felt for jade and the importance of this stone in the development of their civilization are such that every book dealing with Chinese art must devote at least one chapter to it. But before we discuss its strange preeminence—not only as a precious stone, but also as an element in itself—we must explain its nature and specify the various minerals which the term 'jade' includes. And in doing that we must bear in mind the Chinese criteria, from which our own are inevitably derived.

The Chinese name for jade is *yü*. Although it is permissible to suppose that this Chinese term, especially as used in literature, covers a far vaster mineral field than our own, it does actually include three separate minerals: what we call 'jadeite', which is a silicate of soda and aluminium; what we call 'nephrite', a silicate of calcium and magnesium; and what we call 'chloromelanite'. It is the different degree of hardness that differentiates these three types and jadeite is the hardest of the three, although none of them can be scratched by a steel point and all are between the sixth and seventh degree in the scale in which diamonds reach ten degrees and talc is zero. The position of jade in this scale is not very high, but we must not forget that its fibrous structure renders it particularly tough.

The Chinese word for jadeite is *fei-tzui*, and it is from this type of jade that jewels are generally made and it is this type that, more than the other varieties, looks like non-transparent glass. On account of the impurities due to the presence of oxides, its colours range from a beautiful green even more brilliant than that of emeralds, to an almost transparent white and magnificent nuances of lavender and violet. All these shades are frequently found in one and the same block.

Nephrite, which the Chinese call *yü*, may be milky white or as greasy as mutton-fat; or else it may be greyish, olive green (in which case it is called 'celadon jade'), ivory-coloured like butter, more yellow than 'chicken-fat' or as green as spinach. Whereas jadeite is today found mainly in Burma, nephrite comes from Eastern Turkestan and from the western end of Lake Baikal, often in the form of large pebbles. The impetuous River Mekong, on the other hand, carries down towards the sea the valuable *fei-tzui*, but from time immemorial pebbles and small lumps have been stopped long before they reach the Siamese plain. Both nephrite and jadeite have a kind of brownish skin, which the Chinese cutters often leave intact, as a reminder of the material from which their carvings spring. Chloromelanite, on the other hand, is always of a dark green colour, difficult to distinguish at a first glance from nephrite; like the latter, it is mined in Siberia, though there are deposits of both these minerals in the European Alps. It is interesting to note that these European mines have been rediscovered only recently, thus exploding that satisfying theory of a migration of peoples, based on the discovery of implements for the working of jade among the relics of prehistoric European cultures. Jade was also used and esteemed in Mexico and in Peru, where it had a reputation as a therapeutic. As a matter of fact, the words 'jade' and 'nephrite' are both derived from the same part of the human body: the former from the Spanish *ijada*, meaning 'loins', and the latter from the Greek νεφρός, which means 'kidney'. It was, in fact, believed that this stone, taken in the form of powder, had considerable curative value for diseases of the kidneys.

*

The most ancient discoveries on Chinese soil, at Yang Shao, consist of carefully finished objects in jade, evidently destined for sacrificial rites. Among a people so dedicated to the worship of the past, this is sufficient to convince us of the high standing which jade enjoyed for generations. The very characteristics of this mineral, which at a first glance make it seem insignificant, were what had a great attraction for the Chinese, since they coincided with the Chinese conception of virtue. Though apparently soft, it is in reality hard and ever-lasting, and moreover . . . but let us listen to Confucius' reply to that inquisitive and tenacious disciple, one of whose innumerable questions was: 'Why is jade considered so valuable, Master? Is it only on account of its rarity?' To which the Master replied: 'No, that is not the reason. From time immemorial, men have found in jade all the virtues. For is it not soft, smooth and shining like benevolence? Moreover, it is beautiful, robust and compact, like intelligence: it has sharp, but not cutting, edges, like justice, and when it is struck, it emits a long, clear note. It does not try to hide its defects, which do but enhance its beauty, like sincerity. And its substance, found in the mountains and the torrents, shines like

PLATE E. Porcelain bowl. Ming Dynasty, Shuen Te period. Diameter 8¹/₄ inches (21 cm.). *Collection of Marchese G. Litta-Modignani, Capalbio.*

the heavens. It is therefore right that all should love it, as all should love duty and truth.'

In more recent times jade has acquired another quality, though of more dubious moral value. The very nature of this mineral makes it peculiarly suitable for that game of chance which provides the Chinese with a source of powerful emotion. A lump of *fei-tzui* as big as a chair may conceal a coloured kernel no bigger than a nut, but ten times more valuable than the whole of the rest of the block. The lump, covered with earth and the thin skin that millennia of contact with earth and water have formed around it, is bargained for on the strength of a nick cut into it, of a sliver no more than two or three inches deep, not unlike the little cuts the melon-sellers make to show the freshness of the red pulp inside. At Peking there were dealers who made their living out of this dubious activity, running risks comparable with those of a racehorse-owner and a book-maker combined, since they often succeeded in winning over even the most experienced foreign dealers, who, if asked about a purchase which almost inevitably turned out disastrously, were ready to swear that these men possessed the gift of finding out what was inside the lumps with the same ease with which they knew how to estimate the greed of their victims.

The procedure followed in the *dénouement* has remained unchanged throughout the centuries. The lumps were cut by two children who worked a metal saw kept damp by means of a mixture of water and an abrasive agent. The 'slices' of the required dimensions were then hung on the end of a pole, on which stones acted as counterpoises to make the working of the material easier. A number of rotating discs of varying dimensions were then placed on the pole, and finally a set of drills of the kind used by dentists. All these implements were kept fully effective by the same abrasive (sundry compounds of carbonate and silex) and the necessary power was provided by the legs of the artisan controlling two levers, which pulled cords running round the axes of the discs and drills. Only when the finished article was being polished (sometimes after years of carving), by means of wheels and little discs soaked in resin, was it possible to discover the real value of the material that had been purchased, even if, by dipping it in water during the early phases of the cutting, it had been possible to form an idea of the extent to which one had been swindled.

At the time of the SHANG-YIN DYNASTY (?1766–1122? B.C.), however, we may suppose that other criteria prevailed, inspired by the deep ritualistic feeling proper to those religious fanatics, and also because the material they used was different, having been known in China only for a short time, and of such a kind that it could not conceal the exciting surprises to be found in *fei-tzui*. This valuable element was used for the fashioning of a great variety of articles for ceremonial and ritual use—daggers and halberds, axes and tablets almost invariably without any decorations, and, more interesting from the point of view of art, animals, birds and mythological creatures carved with great power and skill, precursors not only of the beautiful jade carvings of following periods, but also of the delicate little bronzes of the late Chou and Han Dynasties. Many of these amulets were used for plugging the 'nine orifices' of a corpse, since it was believed that, when used in this way, jade had the property of preventing decomposition.

Some of these articles have human features, a fact which is noteworthy because it is in contrast with the great scarcity of such representations in the bronzes of the same period. Somehow they allow us to discern an intimate element of this ancient civilization, a small revelation of how those people regarded man—as fierce and justly terrifying. Little articles of a similar kind were sewn on to the clothing of the dead, in order to keep them in proper ritual order (Plate 56).

It was in jade, and at this time, that the *pi* and the *ts'ung* made their first appearance. The former were round discs with large holes in the centre, representing the female element, while the latter were shaped like elongated cubes pierced by a round hole and represented the male element. To start with, these two symbols had no decorations, but we shall see how, later on, they were used as a basis for very fine decorative compositions.

During the CHOU PERIOD (1122–221 B.C.) jade remained the ritualistic material *par excellence*, and during most of this era there are no features enabling us to distinguish the articles produced from those of the preceding Dynasty. Daggers and other articles, which the Shangs had produced without decorations, were now embellished, often in a bold and vivacious manner, by craftsmen ready to give a decorative function to any element whatsoever. The production of small animals continued, but it is not until the last years of the Chou Dynasty (known until a few years ago as the 'Period of the Warring States') that we find that really outstanding skill which was capable of transforming natural forms into powerful, vigorous and profoundly beautiful stylizations for decorative purposes. As an example of this artistic trend, it would be difficult to find anything comparable with the magnificent *pi* reproduced in Plate 57.

By the end of the Chou period jade was being used not only as a personal ornament, but also as a symbol of rank and profession. Notwithstanding this, it was still considered with profound respect, and even with veneration. The pieces of raw material were still subjected to close study by the craftsmen, who tried to avoid, as far as possible, altering their natural shape. This respectful attitude, this voluntary submission to the laws of Nature in the transformation of one of her elements into valuable objects, was, as we have seen, one of the basic principles of the Chinese. 'That neither man nor beast may be able to distinguish the articles made by the potter when they are found scattered in the forest': that was the criterion of the Sung artists and the aim which inspired every craftsman in China when he began working on those materials that Nature had placed within reach of his hand.

*

The decadence of jade from a purely religious material to one accessible to all culminated at the beginning of the HAN DYNASTY (206 B.C.–A.D. 220). By now it had become an ornamental stone used to decorate furniture, swords, sheaths and armour. For personal adornment preference was given to finely carved animals made of carefully selected material, which were worn either as jewels or as amulets.

The Imperial family could indulge in large blocks of the still valuable mineral, carved to represent the

PLATE F. Painting on silk: « The Tribute Horse » (detail). Sung Dynasty.
Metropolitan Museum of Art, New York.

symbols of good auspices for the duration of Imperial rule: the horse and the bear. The Chinese annals even record as an actual fact the appearance of a jade horse every time a noble and virtuous man ascended the celestial throne (Plate 58).

*

During the following centuries jade was worked only by artisans—in the sense we Westerners give to the word. They contributed to the enhancement of the value of this stone, simply by improving the technique of carving and opening up new sources of supply. Under the T'ANG DYNASTY (A.D. 618–906) jade became the ideal, and much abused, medium for every kind of embellishment, in tune with the rich orchestration of this glorious era. The courtesans played lutes and flutes made of jade before retiring to jade beds, after removing the jade hairpins from their *coiffure*. To keep pace with the enormous demand, the artistic element in the production of this time was inevitably neglected. Not until the SUNG DYNASTY (960–1279) did a certain restraint become apparent, which gave jade the characteristic typical of the whole period. The great era of ceramics drew inspiration from jade in its search for colours and surfaces, but the noble material undoubtedly returned the compliment by drawing inspiration from the ceramic forms.

*

The MING DYNASTY (1368–1644), after all this grace and simplicity, saw a return to T'ang mannerisms and also introduced, for the first time, but definitely, that beautiful quality of nephrite known as 'white jade' or 'mutton-fat jade'. The vogue for carvings of animals became ever greater, a vogue which was to last down to our own times and, in its smaller groups, reveals that great love for the animal kingdom which, as in the bronzes of the late Chou and Han periods, formed part of the Shang-Yin heritage (Plate 59).

The great discovery of *fei-tzui* was made during the CH'ING DYNASTY (1644–1911). Though they are elaborate, large and sometimes also beautiful, the K'ang Hsi and Chien Lung pieces would not be deserving of mention if it were not for the beauty of the material used and the skill with which the patches of colour in the block are exploited and arranged (Frontispiece).

White or 'mutton-fat' jade is still carved today and is very popular among the Chinese, but if one wishes to find really fine pieces among the huge number produced, it is necessary to search with determination. Large pieces of spinach-coloured jade were brought to the Imperial palace at this time and, together with white or whitish pieces, surrounded the aesthete Chien Lung, while he wrote poems about jade and sometimes even incised them on jade.

It must, however, be admitted that the importance of these objects lies in the value of the material and the long time needed for making them. A proof of this is that modern pieces fetch prices not very much lower than those of similar pieces made two or even three hundred years ago, which are rapidly disappearing from the market, while the Chinese authorities of today still permit the manufacture of objects in jade and their sale against 'hard' currency. The trade is a flourishing one. From the pockets of rich Western capitalists, the money passes into the safes of their declared enemies. And what is the moral to be drawn from this, when we consider that such pieces are bought more as a capital investment than to satisfy a desire for beauty?

CHAPTER NINE

Lacquer

THE word 'lacquer' recalls to the minds of many
people another word, Coromandel, and both evoke
the dark splendour of a sumptuously decorated screen.
Let us therefore try to throw a little light on the
obscurity surrounding this name, leaving till later all
consideration of those aspects of the material which
have made of it an artistic medium.

Coromandel is the geographical name of that portion
of the Indian coast which served as an assembly point
for all the merchandise that the East India Company
imported from the Far East in order to ship it to the
European markets. Thence came the first Chinese
screens to reach the West and, since they took its name,
it was believed for a long time that they were of Indian
manufacture. Towards the end of the seventeenth
century, in the reign of the Emperor K'ang Hsi,
Chinese fashion favoured screens consisting of thin
panels carefully made, covered with a substance
resembling gum and derived from the bark of a tree
(*Rhus vernicifera*), which was cultivated in China to the
south of the Yellow River. This whitish and transparent substance—lacquer—has poisonous properties
and is harmful to the skin, for which reason it could
only be handled by experts; in addition to this it has the
property of 'drying' in a damp place. Each new coating
of lacquer was carefully applied on top of the preceding
coating, well dried (or rather allowed to harden) and
then pared smooth. The layer obtained by means of

these successive applications was incised and the surfaces thus exposed were delicately painted or gilded. Lacquer (which the Chinese call *ch'i*) also has the property of absorbing colours perfectly: cinnabar turns it to a brilliant and very beautiful red, iron oxide or simple exposure to the air to a shiny black, gamboge to yellow and a mixture of cinnabar and iron oxide to brown. After 1930 the United States demanded lacquers in other colours, especially white, and the Chinese, always quicker in the commercial field than any other nation, hastened to produce articles in white and green lacquer. Nevertheless, certain experts, partly because it was difficult to give to such articles the degree of hardness typical of lacquer, put forward the hypothesis that they were made of rubber, a substance even more sensitive to colours than lacquer.

It must be admitted that some of the incised lacquer screens of the K'ang Hsi period achieve a high degree of beauty, thanks to the still virile draughtsmanship of the time. But this beauty gradually diminished, curiously enough, in proportion to the size of the figures in the decorations—until forgers got to work and restored to the personages on their screens that boldness of conception and those dimensions which the Chinese have always taken as a basis for dating them.

A technique very similar to that we have just described, but used for smaller objects, is frequently found in the MING DYNASTY (1368–1644). Boxes, chair-arms, small articles of furniture, vases, small screens, were robustly and beautifully engraved during the reigns of Yung Lo and Shuen Te, from cartoons executed by the competent Imperial artists, who also worked for the manufacturers of porcelain and the weavers of tapestries. Careful stylistic comparisons leave no room for doubt as to the existence of such artists in the service of the Emperor, and their beautiful designs were transferred to various materials for the use of the Imperial family. The decadence of the artistic value of these designs becomes clearly apparent towards the end of the Dynasty, though the richness of the materials and the elegance of the forms remain.

Many of these incised lacquer articles are of a cinnabar-red colour. On wooden or metal foundations there are sometimes as many as a hundred coatings of lacquer; the decorations, deeply engraved, are usually floral or else symbols of one of the religions, but articles made for Imperial use also display magnificent and virile dragons or dynamic phoenixes. The beauty of these pieces had a Baroque naturalism, achieved by means of elaborate drawing and engraving. But there is also a certain charm emanating from the richness of so many layers of a material which, while it can become as hard as stone, contrives to retain its own peculiar mellow softness.

This system of lacquering with many deeply engraved layers lasted throughout the Ming and Ching dynasties. After degenerating steadily in form and design, it finally debased itself to the level of the horrors created by Western taste. Lacquer, in fact, was so much to the taste of Madame de Pompadour that she seems to have devoted all her spare time to collecting it, the collection being now in the Louvre. Nothing, alas!, could be more deserving of the deprecatory name of 'chinoiserie' than this recent production of lacquer.

*

PLATE 59. Stag with a boy, in jade. Ming Dynasty. Length 6 inches (15 cm.).
Collection of Mrs. Victor Murray, London.

PLATE 60. Sword in lacquered
sheath. Late Chou or early
Han period. Length 31 1/2 in-
ches (80 cm.). *Collection of
Mr. & Mrs. F. Low-Beer,
New York.*

PLATE 61. Inside of a lacquer lid. *Ch'angsha*. Late Chou or early Han period.
Diameter 11 ⁵/₈ inches (29.5 cm.). *Collection of Mr. & Mrs. F. Low-Beer, New York.*

PLATE 62. Lacquer bowl (detail of the inside), *Lolang* (Korea).
Early Han Dynasty. *Musée Guimet, Paris*.

Nevertheless, during the golden age of Chinese artistic achievement, lacquer was by no means neglected. Whereas during the SUNG DYNASTY (960–1279) the *dry* technique, which we shall explain later, was used to obtain forms resembling those of Sung potters and often reproducing them exactly, under the T'ANG DYNASTY (618–906), painting and intarsia-work were used, often with surprisingly beautiful decorative effect. The precious material was used in various ways during this period of splendour. A really striking series of specimens is to be found in the collection at Nara, in Japan, in the so-called Shōsō-in. This notable collection, dating from A.D. 756, was brought together by the widow of a Japanese Emperor of the period and is unfortunately accessible to the public only a few times during the year. Since all the pieces are still in the original building erected to house the collection, one has to arm oneself with an electric torch and much goodwill in order to inspect them. But the effort is more than worth while and the perfect state of preservation of these articles gives us a convincing idea of the glory of the T'angs.

The centres for the production of lacquer during the two periods we have mentioned were in the province of Chekiang. Under the Ming and Ching Dynasties, on the other hand, lacquer articles were produced mainly at Peking and in Foochow.

From the years between the end of the CHOU PERIOD and the end of the HAN DYNASTY (about 500 B.C.–A.D. 220) we have lacquered articles of a form and design fully deserving the epithet 'exquisite'. Most of these were discovered only recently in various parts of Eastern Asia, especially in the province of Hunan

(Ch'angsha) and at Lolang in Korea. Despite the distance separating them and the diversity of the regions in which they were discovered (some of the articles come from Loyang and even from Outer Mongolia), they reveal a surprising affinity, which only serves to render still deeper the mystery surrounding them. Nevertheless, these objects have proved to be of great interest for the students of things Chinese, one reason being that they confirm the statements in the Chinese annals, whereas Western scientific research excluded the idea that the Chinese could have used lacquer before the Ming Dynasty.

As regards importance and beauty, the most notable of these finds are those made by Japanese scholars at Lolang in Korea, on the southern bank of the River Tatung. They consist of bowls, boxes, little tables, combs and other household requisites in black or red lacquer, decorated with yellow and green pigments, which for the most part have unfortunately deteriorated owing to the passage of time. Articles have also been found with gold and silver intarsia-work, while many pieces bear the date of manufacture and also give precise information as to the Imperial workshop in which they were produced and the names of all the artisans who contributed to their making. But the strange fact is that many of the pieces bearing such inscriptions are almost completely without decorations, whereas the most beautiful and sumptuously decorated have no inscriptions at all. Many suggestions have been put forward to explain this fact, the most plausible being that made by Mr. Fritz Low-Beer, the great expert and collector of Chinese lacquer, who maintains that only the minor products of the Imperial workshops ever reached Korea (at that time no more than a Chinese colony), while the finest pieces provided with inscriptions remained nearer the Court, and have since been lost owing to the inadequate systems of excavation already deplored. According to this theory, the more richly decorated articles, but lacking inscriptions, found at Lolang came from private workshops, exempted from the bureaucratic obligation to give such elaborate indications, the aim of which was probably to enable the eventual responsibility to be ascertained, and these workshops then exported them to the wealthy colony for the benefit of private purchasers. Nevertheless there still remains the unsolved mystery, so worrying for the inveterate searchers after beauty, of the high quality of the genuine Imperial articles (Plate 62).

The pieces found at Lolang and known to have been made in Szechwan are of somewhat later date than those found in China, properly speaking. But their forms and decorations, though perhaps more graceful, are still vigorous and full of life. The famous lacquered basket, mentioned in the chapter on painting (and now a trophy in the hands of the Northern Koreans), belongs, like the other Lolang finds, to the Han Dynasty.

Nevertheless, while in the case of the piece mentioned above the lacquer covered a basket of plaited strands, in most of the Lolang finds the technique is different and rather ingenious. In this technique, known as that of dry lacquer, the lacquer serves, so to speak, as a foundation. A thin cloth, sometimes stretched on wooden hoops, is impregnated with liquid lacquer until the desired shape has been obtained. If the outline is complicated, as in the case of statues, this is done by making the impregnated cloth adhere to models made of wood or ceramics, which are then removed. When the form, now empty, is as hard as it should be, it is covered with innumerable layers of lacquer dyed to the colour required with cinnabar or rust, after which the decoration begins. The shapes of the Lolang utensils are all extremely elegant and the decorations generally reveal a rarely equalled degree of decorative inventiveness.

The pieces brought to light at Ch'angsha, on the other hand, are attributed to the period between the last years of the Chou and the Han Dynasty. Though on the whole coarser than the Lolang pieces, they display forms of stylization which are ingenious and full of imagination. These articles also differ from those of Lolang in the choice of foundation, which in nearly every case is wood. Unfortunately, as a result of their long immersion in water, many of these exquisite specimens have suffered irreparable damage because they were put to dry immediately after they had been disinterred. In most cases the wood foundation buckled and shrank, causing the lacquer surface to crack and then peel off. Today in the museums many fine specimens are kept constantly damp, to prevent their destruction—in view of the fragility of this material, so delicate and at the same time so lasting (Plate 61).

We have no information as to where the pieces found at Ch'angsha were made. Although Szechwan (the province where, as we have seen, the Lolang pieces were produced) borders on Hunan, political conditions immediately preceding the Han period suggest that they may have been produced locally at Ch'angsha. Among the states at war after the fall of the Chous, the State of

PLATE 63. Anthropomorphic figure, in wood. *Ch'angsha*, 4th or
5th century B. C. *British Museum, London.*

PLATE 64. Back of a lacquer *Pi-pa* (lute). T'ang Dynasty.
Intarsia work in silver. *Shōsō-in Nara*.

PLATE 65. Surface of a panel in engraved cinnabar lacquer. Yung Lo period. Ming Dynasty. 47 1/4 × 31 1/2 inches (120 × 80 cm.). *Collection of Mr. & Mrs. F. Low-Beer, New York.*

PLATE 66. Two screen panels engraved in lacquer (Coromandel). Height 78³/₄ inches (200 cm.). K'ang Hsi period.
Victoria & Albert Museum, London.

Lu, of which Ch'angsha was the capital, offered more resistance than the others to the unification undertaken by the Ch'in Emperor. Very interesting wooden sculptures have been found there which might indicate a local development not only in artistic but also in religious matters, a development which did not spread to the other provinces of the Empire until the advent of the Hans. But this, too, is a dangerous hypothesis. If no lacquered articles have been found in the environs of the Han capitals, for which the greater part of them must certainly have been intended, how many may still be hidden in that area? And how many of them might upset the hypotheses we have made about the long-tongued human figure found at Ch'angsha? It is supposed that, starting from Ch'angsha, this symbol of fertility crossed India and Siberia and finally arrived in Jutland, France, Yugoslavia and Latium. But in time the soil of Honan might also prove that Ch'angsha was merely its last stopping-place before it crossed the mountains and descended into the Western plains (Plate 63).

*

We have thus seen how wood came to be used as a foundation for lacquer during the last years of the Chous. The decorations on the magnificent lacquer scabbard (Plate 60) were first carved on wood and then covered with lacquer, not only in order to embellish them, but also to protect the very fine intaglio work. On the other hand the dry lacquer, of which the sheath itself is made, is intended not only to give splendour and elegance to this implement of war, but also to make it lighter.

There is no doubt that, at the beginning, lacquer was used by the Chinese as a functional element to make ceramics and wood impermeable to water and air and thus make the preservation of food possible; later, when the technique of 'dry' lacquer had been evolved, light statues, easy to handle, were made for carrying in processions; and lastly, lacquer served to give a lasting brilliance and protection to perishable materials, whether in war or in peace. Nowadays the tendency is to believe that the curious black intarsias forming part of the decorative elements on certain Shang bronzes are simply lacquer, which would mean that even in those days those surprising men were aware of the imperishable quality of this substance. If that were not the case, they would certainly not have used lacquer together with a noble and lasting material like bronze. The truth is that lacquer is probably as old as Chinese civilization itself.

*

But our thoughts return to the lacquer sheath and the quality of Chinese culture rather than to its age. We like to imagine this lovely object hooked to a soldier's belt, hanging on the flank of a warrior so noble that he preferred to have a beautiful rather than a brutal weapon to adorn his person on the battlefield.

CHAPTER TEN

Fabrics, Silver, Jewels

THE ancient Greeks used to call the Chinese *Seres*, from the Chinese word *Ssu*, meaning 'silk'. In fact, for our own ancestors the Chinese were the very distant manufacturers of that exquisite and valuable material which denoted the social rank of those who wore it, as mink does today. But even in this field the over-zealous student will bring out his little story, which his sceptical colleagues are bound to take into consideration, if only on account of the originality of its conception. A certain Hans Rebel, in fact, maintains that the idea of spinning the cocoons of certain larvae is not of Chinese origin, but comes from the Aegean island of Kos. There, as in Assyria and India, *bombasine* was made and worn in days which Professor Rebel, in 1927, considered very ancient, namely at the end of the second millennium B.C. Nowadays we are bound to consider this date as much less ancient, since we have to refer it to the most recent discoveries of neolithic Chinese earthenware bearing on its surface clear traces of woven silk, as well as of fragments of spindles in earthenware, not very different from those used today. Nevertheless, even Professor Rebel gives the Chinese credit for developing the manufacture of silk and domesticating the silk-worm, and for our part we are grateful to him for having conclusively proved that, in the matter of silk, the Chinese had established business relations with the West long before Pliny complained of the high cost of this material and before the Greek philosophers of the fourth century B.C. had tried to explain the technique of weaving it to their disciples.

The age-old, innate business sense of the Chinese and, to an even greater extent, their skill and patience and that particular genius for organization necessary in the production of silk, had as a result that the manufacture of this material remained their own secret and privilege for many centuries. About the middle of the first millennium B.C. the secret was smuggled out of China and reached Constantinople, presumably thanks to some Persian monks who concealed a few silkworms' eggs in their hollow mendicants' staffs.

There is no doubt that the Shang-Yins and the Chous used silk for their clothes. Silk fibres and other traces of the woven fabric impressed on bronzes have been found in Shang-Yin tombs, while in those of the Chous pieces of jade carved in the shape of silkworms have come to light.

The earliest pieces of woven silk hitherto found date, however, from the Han Dynasty. It is interesting to note at this point that the most important discoveries have been made outside the frontiers of China proper, and more precisely along the famous 'Silk Road'. At the beginning of the present century, the great British scientist and explorer Sir Aurel Stein discovered important remains in the Tarim basin, and, earlier still, in the Tun Huang desert. These finds show a very advanced technique of weaving, with decorations of a notable vivacity: animals, the usual *tao-tieh* and fine geometrical designs. Other pieces found in the neighbourhood of Urga, and likewise attributed to the early Han period, are beautifully embroidered.

Pieces of silk dating from the late Han period have

been found at Palmyra, that stubborn adversary of ancient Rome, and also in the Crimea, through which a secondary route for the flourishing trade in silk between China and Rome must have passed. The patterns, beautiful and complicated, remind us of the decorations on bronze mirrors of the period, thus confirming their Chinese origin. It is assumed that, as time went on, the Roman matrons acquired a certain familiarity with the typically Chinese patterns, though there are no proofs of their having had any influence on Roman designs.

*

When we come to the woven fabrics of the T'ang Dynasty, we have to turn to Japan and, more precisely, again to the Shōsō-in collection. There we find specimens of fabrics with typically Chinese decorations printed in the 'batik' manner. On the other hand, Sir Aurel Stein discovered T'ang embroideries in the Tun Huang desert, in the rock temple of the Thousand Buddhas. The famous banner with its marvellous stitching and brilliant colours (red, yellow and black), now in the British Museum, is undoubtedly the finest example of Chinese embroidery dating from a period when the art of design had reached full maturity (Plate 68).

The well-known *k'o ssu* technique, which might be described as a *gobelin* in silk, had already achieved full development by the T'ang period. The Chinese name for it means 'engraved silk'. The designs for these fabrics, incredibly meticulous and precise, were derived from specially made drawings, and often from paintings by ancient or contemporary masters and from calligraphy. In the earliest beautiful specimens, and throughout the whole of the Sung and Ming Dynasties, painting was used only for the tiniest details, the rest being executed by the weaver in accordance with the *gobelin* technique. As time went on, however, under K'ang Hsi and Ch'ien Lung and down to our own times, as the work of the artisans became more and more popular in tone, more and more use was made of painting, which took the place of coloured threads, thus avoiding a great deal of patient toil. But so far no one has succeeded in equalling the perfection of this weaving. If compared with these fabrics as regards the density of warp and woof, the best French *gobelins* seem definitely outclassed. Unfortunately not a single specimen of the great production of *k'o ssu* mentioned in the annals has come down to us and we do not possess enough Sung tapestries and fabrics of other kinds to be able to form an idea of them. We must, however, believe the historians of the time, since there is no doubt that this collateral activity must have formed a worthy accompaniment to the great paintings of the period.

*

It is above all in European cathedrals that we can form an idea of the importance of Yuan and Ming embroidery and weaving. Among the merchandise bought and sold by the Venetian family of Polo there must certainly have been beautiful silks and fine embroideries executed according to patterns supplied by their ecclesiastical customers.

The finest specimens, however, have come to us through the robbers of Ming tombs in the neighbourhood of Peking. In many cases time, the soil and acids have given even greater relief to the beauty of the sumptuous garments in which the Emperors and their relatives had themselves buried. Every bird, every animal, every flower and every plant had its own meaning and conveyed its own message. And on the borders of the vestments stretched the sea with its waves shown in a hundred nuances of colour, never tamed, but always under the watchful eye of the celestial orbit.

Notwithstanding this, and although the Emperor attached great importance to ceremonial and to the robes prescribed by an etiquette which he himself had completely revised, the textiles and embroideries of the Ch'ien Lung period no longer display the vigour of design characteristic of the Ming Dynasty. It may be true that the skill of the artisans, especially in embroidery, reached its zenith in these gorgeous Imperial robes, but his art was definitely in decline—not only as regards design, but also in the colouring.

That is also true of the manufacture of carpets. The annals tell us little about this kind of work, but there is no doubt that the Chinese used to cover their floors with woollen fabrics long before the Han period. This silence on the part of the literary sources is perhaps due to the fact that carpets were looked upon as imported goods, since they were made in the remotest parts of the Empire, in Ninghsia and Mongolia. Be that as it may, a few remnants of carpets were found along the 'Silk Road' by Sir Aurel Stein, and the Shōsō-in collection has interesting specimens executed in a now forgotten technique. Marco Polo expatiates on the carpets and tent-coverings he saw in China and we too have seen Ming carpets, excellent though small, with vigorous designs and still bright colours (red and yellow splashed with scarlet).

*

In the early years of the Chou period precious metals made their first appearance in the repertory of Chinese craftsmen. It is interesting to note that gold and silver were held to be of almost equal value during this and the following Han period, and it was not until Western greed penetrated the Chinese market that the price of the yellow metal began to rise. As we have already seen, both gold and silver were used for intarsia-work on bronzes, but it would seem that the first articles made entirely of these metals were produced during the Chou period. The form and decorations of all the pieces found and attributed to this period, however, were obtained only by casting.

During the late Chou and early Han periods, on the other hand, we find gold wrought with great taste and skill. The pommel of the lacquer sheath reproduced in Plate 60, for example, is decorated with a thin band of gold executed by the technique known to goldsmiths as 'granulé'. Tiny globules of gold are heated to a temperature which allows them to attach themselves to one another without melting and without losing their original roundness. Thus joined together, they form a design of little pellets separated by exquisitely executed spirals. This technique is the same as that used by the Etruscans for their jewels.

PLATE 67. Silk tapestry (k'o-
ssu). 17th century. Height
51¼ inches (130 cm.).
Private collection.

PLATE 68. Banner on linen embroidered in silk. From the Tun-huang caves.
T'ang Dynasty. Height 75 inches (190 cm.). *British Museum, London.*

PLATE 69. Silver bowl. T'ang Dynasty. Diameter 5 7/8 inches (15 cm.).
Collection of Dr. Carl Kempe, Stockholm.

PLATE 70. Gold and silver buckle with turquoise intarsia-work (detail). Late Chou or early Han period. Length 3 inches (7.5 cm.). *Musée Guimet, Paris*

Almost equally delicate is the craftsmanship that can be admired on the hilt of the sword now in the British Museum, forming part of the collection of that pioneer in the study of Chinese art, George Eumorfopoulos. This, too, is attributed to the late Chou period—the period during which began the production of those beautiful buckles rightly considered to be a revelation of the high degree of civilization the Chinese people must have achieved if they insisted upon artistry of this kind for their personal adornment. All the buckles so far found are very elegant, but for some of them this epithet is quite inadequate. The golden shell of the agrafe of Plate 70, chiselled to form the features, ferocious but imposing, of a serpent and fitted over a silver lining, is the work of a great sculptor, while the turquoise intarsia-work and the decorations in gold which set it off are the work of an equally great gold-smith. An interesting feature of this article is the button at the back, designed to fasten the buckle either to the robe or to a leather belt and made by a process generally called *niello*. A reddish paste (of lacquer? or enamel?), not unlike the black substance of the decorations on Shang-Yin bronzes, fills *cloisons*, or compartments, arranged so as to form a decorative pattern. This process, which degenerated fifteen hundred years later into *cloisonné* (another stout supporter of the term *chinoiserie*), is generally supposed to be of Roman origin (Latin *nigellus*). But the buckle we are discussing definitely belongs to the early Han period, if not even to the late Chou.

Buckles have been found made of solid gold with whole portions of them in jade. These must certainly have come from the tombs of princes, like that we have just described, and another buckle, really exquisite and with very fine gold filigree, which came to light at Lolang.

*

It is once again in Shōsō-in that we are able not only to examine and admire, but also to study the production of valuable articles from the T'ang period, thus establishing the chronology of similar articles found elsewhere. Boxes, bowls and small chalices are here found, executed in gold and silver, but in technique and pattern completely different from earlier Chinese styles in decoration. This change, which occurred during the T'ang Dynasty, can also be seen in other fields—in textiles, in lacquer, and in what has been the citadel of Chinese expressiveness, ceramics. But its origin is to be sought in these vessels made of precious metals, since this particular craft was brought to China by the Sassanid refugees from Central Persia, together with what we may call the miniaturistic manner. But though the elegant silver vessels and the clear but vigorous motives were of Persian origin, the Chinese soon mastered them and made them their own. The shape was obtained by hammering and the decorations were engraved with hammer and chisel. Nevertheless, the first process, that of flattening the metal to give it the required shape, is carried out with such skill that modern goldsmiths prefer not to commit themselves regarding the technique followed by their ancient colleagues. On occasions parts of the decorative motives on these silver vessels are gilded to give greater relief. Very interesting indeed is the treatment of animals. The innate love of the

Chinese for Nature's creations found full scope in these representations in miniature. Animals having a proud and stylized aspect which might be termed heraldic are almost always made to look somewhat absurd by the other animals decorating the same article, the latter being executed with humorous naturalism (Plate 69).

*

Under the Ming Dynasty gold became so dear that it could only be used for coins and jewels. In 1936 there appeared on the Peking market a very important assortment of valuable ornaments, which came from tombs of the Ming Emperors, or, more precisely, from that of Shuen Te. The booty was of such size and value that the dealers in such articles, usually so audacious in those carefree times, became somewhat cautious. The best-known foreign dealers were allowed, one by one, to inspect it and to make their offers. But suddenly, one day, the whole collection disappeared. Then came the war and of these precious articles which had aroused a fleeting interest, no trace could be found.

They are re-appearing now, a few at a time, having been dispersed perhaps not so much on account of the vicissitudes of war, but owing to the suspicions of the dealers and collectors through whose hands they have passed in the meantime. The memory of this little collection still lives in the minds of many. Far more than the tapestries and the *cloisonné*, far more than the porcelain and the paintings of the time, the jewels revealed the spirit of a robust and wealthy race, which, while trying to revive the glories of a vanished age, yet strove to achieve a certain originality. One article, in particular, deserves to be remembered. The God of Longevity, once cheerfully confused with the philosopher Lao Tze, here becomes an ear-pendant. His elongated head, once the symbol of genius, is now a sapphire and his visceral regions have the transparency of an emerald. He treads upon clouds of rubies. According to the tomb-robbers, these articles had been buried together with their Imperial owner a hundred years before Cellini executed his famous salt-cellar; and yet, in many respects, they represent the last spasm of China's artistic grandeur.

And that is exactly one of the things the author of the present volume has been trying to say: that true Chinese art is never less than four hundred years old and that those articles which have hitherto been looked upon as typical Chinese *objets d'art* really date from a long interval during which no real art was produced.

This assertion takes us back to the beginning, to the Shang-Yins. Between the end of that cycle, three thousand years ago, and the beginning of the next, China seems to have been artistically stagnant for six centuries. Patience and incalculable vitality: these two fundamental gifts of the Chinese show no signs of exhaustion. Because, to borrow a simile from that Nature which the Chinese love so dearly, China is not a torrent, nor even a river—China is a sea.

BIBLIOGRAPHY

ORIGIN AND HISTORY

Linton, R.: *The Tree of Culture*, New York, 1955.

Eberhard, W.: *Chinas Geschichte*, Berne, 1948.

Latourette, K. S.: *The Chinese*, New York, 1946.

Creel, H. G.: *The Birth of China*, London, 1936.

Fitzgerald, C. P.: *China, a Short Cultural History*, London, 1935.

Andersson, J. G.: *Children of the Yellow Earth*, London, 1934.

Hu Shih: *Religion and Philosophy in Chinese History*, Shanghai, 1931.

Grousset, R.: *Histoire de l'Extrême Orient*, Paris, 1929.

Polo, Marco: *Il Milione* (ed. L. F. Benedetto), Rome, 1934.

THE BRONZES

Foster, K. E.: *A Handbook of Ancient Chinese Bronzes*, Claremont, U.S.A., 1949.

Ch'en, M. C.: 'Style of Chinese Bronzes (*Archives of the Chinese Art Society of America*), 1945–6.

Ackerman, P.: *Ritual Bronzes of Ancient China*, New York, 1945.

Karlgren, B.: 'Remarks on the dating of Early Chinese Bronzes' (*Bulletin of the Museum of Far Eastern Antiquities*), Stockholm, 1946.

'Huai and Han' (*ibidem*), Stockholm, 1941.

'New Studies in Chinese Bronzes' (*ibidem*), Stockholm, 1931.

Some Fecundity Symbols in Ancient China' (*ibidem*), Stockholm, 1931.

Salmony, A.: 'Are there Chinese that pre-date Anyang times?' (*Art in America*), 1939.

Creel, H. G.: 'Notes on Prof. Karlgren's System for dating Chinese Bronzes' (*Journal of the Royal Asiatic Society*), 1936. 'On the Origins of the Manufacture and Decorations of Bronze in the Shang Period' (*Monumenta Serica*), Peking, 1935-6.

Yetts, W. P.: 'The Shang-Yin Dynasty and the Anyang Finds' (*Journal of the Royal Asiatic Society*), London, 1933.

Truebner, J.: *Yu und Kuang*, Leipzig, 1929.

Kuemmel, O.: *Chinesische Bronzen*, Berlin, 1929.

EARTHENWARE AND PORCELAIN

Dexel, T.: *Die Formen Chinesischer Keramik*, Tübingen, 1955.

Cheng, C. T.: 'Building the New, Uncovering the Old' (*East and West*), Rome, 1945.

Jenyns, S.: *Ming Pottery and Porcelain*, London, 1953.

Lindberg, G.: 'Hsing Yao and Ting Yao' (*Bulletin of the Museum of Far Eastern Antiquities*), Stockholm, 1953.

Pope, J.: *Fourteenth Century Blue and White*, Washington, 1952. 'Some Blue and White in Istanbul' (*Transactions of the Oriental Ceramic Society*), London, 1950-1.

Karlbeck, O.: 'Proto-porcelain and Yueh Ware' (*Transactions of the Oriental Ceramic Society*), London, 1949-50.

Ingram, Sir H.: 'A New Approach to Early Chinese Ceramics' (*Oriental Art*), 1948.

Hiney, W. B.: *The Ceramic Art of China and Other Countries of the Far East*, London, 1945.

Brankston, A. D.: *Early Ming Wares of Ching-te Chen*, Peking, 1938.

Hobson, R. L.: 'Yueh Ware and Northern Celadon' (*Transactions of the Oriental Ceramic Society*), London, 1936-7.

David, Sir Percival: 'Some Notes on Pi-se Yao' (*Eastern Art*), 1929.

Hetherington, A. L.: *The Early Ceramic Wares of China*, London, 1922.

D'Entrecolles, Père: *Lettres Edifiantes et Curieuses*, 1712.

SCULPTURE

Rowland, D., Jr.: *Art in East and West*, New York, 1955.

Priest, Alan: *Chinese Sculpture in the Metropolitan Museum*, New York, 1943.

Warner, L.: *The Long Old Trail in China*, London, 1938.

Karlbeck, O.: 'Anyang Marble Sculptures' (*Bulletin of the Museum of Far Eastern Antiquities*), Stockholm, 1935.

Tizac, H. d'A.: *La Sculpture Chinoise*, Paris, 1931.

Sirén, O.: *Chinese Sculpture from the Fifth to the Fourteenth Century*, London, 1925.

Pelliot, P.: *Les Grottes de Touen-houang*, Paris, 1914–24.

PAINTING

Giuganino, A.: *Introduzione al Catalogo della Mostra d'Arte Cinese della Città di Venezia*, Venice, 1954.

Priest, A.: *Aspects of Chinese Painting*, New York, 1954.

Suzuki, D. T.: *Essays in Zen Buddhism*, London, 1950.

Contag, V.: *Die beiden Steine*, Brunswick, 1950.

Dubosc, J. P.: *Great Painters of the Ming and Ching Dynasties*, New York, 1949.

Cohn, W.: *Chinese Painting*, London, 1948.

Sakanishi, S.: *The Spirit of the Brush*, London, 1939.

Sickman, L.: 'Notes on Later Chinese Painting' (*Parnassus*), 1939.

Sirén, O.: *History of Later Chinese Painting*, London, 1938.
   The Chinese on the Art of Painting, Peking, 1936.
   History of Early Chinese Painting, London, 1933.
Harada, J.: *A Pageant of Chinese Painting*, Tokyo, 1936.
Ferguson, J. C.: *Chinese Painting*, Chicago, 1927.
Waley, A.: *Introduction to the Study of Chinese Painting*, London,
   1923.
Fry, R.: *Vision and Design*, London, 1920.

THE IVORIES

Prodan, M.: *Certain Ming Ivories*, Peking, 1942.
Sowerby, A. de C.: *Chinese Ivory Carving, Ancient and Modern*,
   Shanghai, 1934.
Laufer, B.: *Ivory in China*, Chicago, 1925.

JADE

David, M.: *Les Jades du Musée Guimet*, Paris, 1948.
Salmony, A.: *Carved Jades of Ancient China*, Berkeley (Cali-
   fornia), 1938.
Nott, S. C.: *Chinese Jade throughout the Ages*, London, 1936.
Goette, J.: *Jade Lore*, Shanghai, 1936.
Laufer, B.: *Jade*, Chicago, 1912.

LACQUER

Salmony, A.: *Antler and Tongue*, Ascona (Switzerland), 1954.
Low-Beer, F.: 'Chinese Lacquer of the Early Fifteenth
   Century' (*Bulletin of the Museum of Far Eastern Antiquities*),
   Stockholm, 1950.
   '*Zu dem Dekor der Han-Lacke*' (*Wiener Beiträge zur Kunst-
   und Kulturgeschichte Asiens*), Vienna, 1937.

Maenchen-Helfen, O.: *Zur Geschichte der Lackkunst in China*, Vienna, 1937.

Seguy, E. A.: *Les laques de Coromandel*, Paris, 1923.

Bonanni, F.: *Trattato sopra la Vernice detta comunemente Cinese*, Bologna, 1786.

FABRICS, SILVER, JEWELS

Priest, A.: *Costumes from the Forbidden City*, New York, 1945.

Hedin, S.: *The Silk Road*, London, 1938.

Stein, Sir Aurel: *Serindia. Report of Excavations in Central Asia and Westernmost China*, Oxford, 1921.

Andrews, F. H.: *Ancient Chinese Figured Silks excavated by Sir Aurel Stein at Ruined Sites of Central Asia*, London, 1920.

Gyllenswaerd, B.: *Chinese Gold and Silver in the C. Kempe Collection*, Stockholm, 1953.

Priest, A.: 'Chinese Jewelry' (*Bulletin of the Metropolitan Museum of Art*), New York, 1944.

Andersson, J. G.: 'The Goldsmith in Ancient China' (*Bulletin of the Museum of Far Eastern Antiquities*), Stockholm, 1955.

LIST OF PERIODICALS DEALING WITH
CHINESE ART

Archives of the Chinese Art Society of America (New York).

Artibus Asiae (Ascona, Switzerland).

Bulletin of the Museum for Far Eastern Antiquities (Stockholm).

Bulletin de l'École Française (Hanoi).

East and West (Rome).

Études Asiatiques (Paris).

Monumenta Serica (Peking, now Tokyo).

Transactions of the Oriental Ceramic Society (London).

Wiener Beiträge zur Kunst- und Kulturgeschichte Asiens (Vienna).

INDEX

Heng An, 125
ho, 69, 76
Honan, 83, 84, 92, 93, 96, 101, 105, 109, 122
Hong Kong, 91, 173
Hopei, 105, 108, 122, 178
Hsia Kuei, 161
Hsiang Sheng-Mo, 166
hsien, 70
Hsüan Te, 111
Hsüan Tsung, 56
Huai, 78
Huang Chüan, 154
Huang Ho (Yellow River), 172
Huang Kung-Wang, 163
Hui-hsien, 92, 123
Hui Tsung, 160
Hunan, 193
Hung Wu, 60
Huo, K'iu Ping, 121

IMMORTALS, The, 22, 134, 177
Imperial Canal, The, 53
India, 55, 123, 172, 197, 199
Indians, 53, 123, 124, 126, 130
iron oxide, 90
Istanbul, 103, 111
Ivory, 171–9

JADE, 80, 99, 102, 117, 180–9
Jadeite, 180, 181
Japan, 54, 109, 151, 155, 193, 201
Japanese, 62, 104, 108, 174, 194
Jen Jen-Fa, 162
Jesuits, 168, 169, 170
Juchow, 101
Jutland, 197
Ju-yao, 101, 102

K'AIFENG, 58, 102
Kakemono, 136

Karlgren, Professor Bernhard, 77, 78
K'ang Hsi, 114, 166, 167, 169, 178, 188, 190, 191, 202
Kansu, 37
Kao Tsung, 55
kaolin, 83, 86, 95
Khotan, 151
Kiangsi, 96, 105, 106, 110
Kiangsu, 95, 105, 109
ko, 71
Korea, 50, 53, 95, 106, 151, 194, 195
Kos, 199
K'o ssu, 201, 202
Ko-yao, 102, 115
Ku, 69, 78
Ku An, 163
Kuan-hsiu, 154
Kuan Tao-Shen, 162, 165
Kuan-yao, 102
kuei, 69, 78
Ku Kai-Chih, 148, 149
K'un-Ts'an, 169
Kung K'ai, 162
Kung Tzu (Confucius), 45
Kuo Hsi, 157
Kwan Yin, 124, 177

LACQUER, 191–8
Lang-Shih-Ning (Castiglione), 170
Lao Tzu, 45, 47, 78, 208
lead oxide, 86, 94, 95
lead silicate, 93
lei, 70
li, 69
Liang Kai, 161
Li Chin, 61
Li K'an, 163
Li Lung-Mien, 159
Li Po, 55
Li Shih-Min, 54, 55

217

218

219